CONRAD'S LINGARD TRILOGY

THE ORIGINS OF MODERNISM:
GARLAND STUDIES IN BRITISH LITERATURE
(VOL. 1)

GARLAND REFERENCE LIBRARY
OF THE HUMANITIES
(VOL. 1284)

THE ORIGINS OF MODERNISM: GARLAND STUDIES IN BRITISH LITERATURE

Series editor: Todd K. Bender

CONRAD'S LINGARD TRILOGY
Empire, Race, and Women
in the Malay Novels

Heliéna Krenn

GARLAND PUBLISHING, INC. • NEW YORK & LONDON
1990

Library of Congress Cataloging-in-Publication Data

Krenn, Heliéna, 1932–
    Conrad's Lingard trilogy: empire, race, and women in the Malay
novels / Heliéna Krenn.
        p.   cm. — (The origins of modernism: Garland studies in
British literature; vol. 1) (Garland reference library of the
humanities; vol. 1284)
    Includes bibliographical references.
    ISBN 0-8240-5798-8 (alk. paper)
    1. Conrad, Joseph, 1857–1924—Knowledge—Malay Archipelago.
2. Conrad, Joseph, 1857–1924—Characters—Tom Lingard. 3. Conrad,
Joseph, 1857–1924. Outcast of the islands. 4. Conrad, Joseph,
1857–1924. Almayer's folly. 5. Conrad, Joseph, 1857–1924. Rescue.
6. Malay Archipelago in literature. 7. Race relations in
literature. 8. Imperialism in literature. 9. Women in literature.
I. Title. II. Series. III. Series: Origins of modernism; vol. 1.
PR6005.O4Z76345   1990
823'.912—dc20   90–31443
                                                            CIP

Printed on acid-free, 250-year-life paper
Manufactured in the United States of America

SERIES EDITOR'S PREFACE

The Modernist Movement, characterized by the works of T.S. Eliot, James Joyce, Virginia Woolf, William Faulkner, and writers of similar stature, dominated Anglo-American literature for some fifty years following World War I. By the time the United States emerged from its military involvement in Indo-China in the 1970s, the Modernist Movement had disintegrated into Post-Modernism. High Modernism's most proud claim was that it would "make it new," that it represented a radical and sudden break with previous cultural traditions. We now see this claim to be false. Nowhere is Modernism more derivative than in its claim to radical novelty. The Modernist "revolution" of the twentieth century is best seen as the culmination of ideology developing in the late nineteenth century. This series of books is devoted to the study of the origins of Modernism in the half-century between the Franco-Prussian War and the First World War, from the death of Dickens to the roaring twenties and the Lost Generation.

As drama is the center of the literature of the Elizabethan Age, so criticism is the focus of the Modernist Age. Modernist writers worked in an environment of university and school curricula more introspective, self-conscious, and cannibalistic than ever before. How did the philosophical and pedagogical system supporting Modernism develop? What part does feminism play in the struggle for literary domination? How do changing systems of patronage and the economy of literature influence Modernism as a vastly expanded reading public is eventually augmented by cinema, radio, and television as consumers of literature? Do the roots of cultural pluralism within English literature recede back to the Victorian era? When English is used as the vehicle for expression of American, Canadian, Australian, or Indian culture; or for Afro-American, Hispano-American, Asian-American, or Amero-Indian culture, where do the origins of this eclectic pluralism lie?

We believe that there are two important groups of writers essential to the development of Modernism: (1) Gerard Manley Hopkins and the circle of his correspondents (Robert Bridges, Coventry Patmore, Canon Richard Watson Dixon, and related figures) and (2) the circle of writers surrounding Joseph Conrad (Ford Madox Ford, Henry James, Stephen Crane, and others). We especially encourage the further study of these two groups as foundation stones for the Modernist Movement, but there are many other sources important to its development.

Todd K. Bender
University of Wisconsin

PREFACE TO THIS VOLUME

If the exiled Polish sea-captain we know as Joseph Conrad (1857–1924) had not begun to write fiction in 1889 in English, a language remote from his mother tongue and foreign to his childhood, the whole shape and history of the Modernist Revolution in literature would be quite different. Heliéna Krenn explores that creative moment, that crucial episode, when Conrad first set pen to paper. Conrad's first two novels, *Almayer's Folly* (1895) and *An Outcast of the Islands* (1896), as well as *The Rescue* (1920) are set in the Malay Archipelago and Bornea and share common characters. Conrad's *The Rescue* was initiated soon after *Almayer's Folly* and *An Outcast of the Islands*, but not completed for many years, held in abeyance while the great works of his career unfolded. These three volumes, all linked by the character of Captain Tom Lingard and his world, form a triology bracketing the beginning and ending of Conrad's career. As Krenn argues, "It was the Malay Archipelago with its truths about human life dimmed by the mists of its jungles and waterways that started Conrad on his career as a novelist." We might imagine the Lingard trilogy as a frame containing those other great works by Conrad concerning the colonial experience and imperialist ambitions of European nations, *Lord Jim* (1900) and "Heart of Darkness" (1899). If we see "Heart of Darkness" enfolded into *Lord Jim*, and both enclosed in the Lingard trilogy, then the narrator's explanation in "Heart of Darkness" (that Marlow's tales carry their meaning not "inside like a kernel, but outside enveloping the tale [like] . . . misty halos") becomes a direction for careful readers to look to the Lingard books well.

Krenn argues powerfully that the Lingard trilogy must be read as a unit. Actions in one book appear to have their motives in another. Characters develop coherently from story to story. The politics and history of the peoples in each setting are consistent and gather force with the flow of events. One book will reveal a covert plot masked in the overt plot stated in another. Imagery is incremental across the trilogy: light versus dark, the wilderness, the river, the floating log. These transtextual arguments are not only fresh and compelling by themselves, they also provide a new approach to other texts by Conrad.

If Conrad's art is rooted in his encounter with the colonial and imperialistic world, we come to the two most hotly argued issues in current criticism of Conrad: Is Conrad fundamentally racist and sexist? Framing the Lingard trilogy as a point of reference and applying a transtextual approach sheds new light on such questions. Krenn is surely correct in linking the marginalization of the female and the colonial theme. The marriage of the half-caste Joanna to the Dutchman Willems parallels the female and the colonized in many dimensions: the economic exploitation, the feeling of dirtiness and sloth, the sense of burden, the sense of cultural and intellectual inferiority. Such illuminating parallels recur throughout the trilogy. Moreover, Krenn's fresh application of lexicographical research to keywords, such as "savage," allows her to explore more carefully the charges that Conrad is racist or sexist than has been done previously. Again, her approach is transtextual, taking a word and tracing its actual denotation and connotation over the trilogy to see how Conrad actually employs the word, so constructing a temporary lexicon for a few key terms in this author's vocabulary. The lexicographical method is a powerful new tool and its advantages should be apparent to all serious scholars.

In reading Conrad, we must not neglect the very obvious. Conrad was polyglot. He turned away from his mother tongue and chose to create his fictions very laboriously in English, which was a language he acquired mainly as an adult. Before Conrad there are few, if any, writers of distinction in the canon of English literature whose native tongue is not English. After Conrad, any undergraduate can name a half-dozen. The use of English as a vehicle to crystallize cultural experiences which are not confined to the British Isles or the English-speaking world, the great sweep of English into the position of the global trade-language, can be seen as the major development of our century, although as yet insufficiently recognized and described. Krenn's study is a step toward that global placement of Conrad's work necessary in the revision of our more parochial, traditional literary history.

The style in which Conrad tells his tales, foregrounding the mental process, presenting an apparent vacuity at the center of language, capturing the raw impression and the process of ratiocination, the practice of "delayed decoding"—in short, everything that Ford Madox Ford meant by the term "literary Impressionism"—can also be traced in the Lingard trilogy. Krenn's treatment of narrative time, imagery, and open plot structures is a useful step toward a definition of the Impressionist Revolution in literature.

Todd K. Bender

CONTENTS

ACKNOWLEDGMENTS

I am indebted to many literary scholars who by their publications have stimulated my interest in the issues and questions that have led to this study.

I am grateful to the Department of English of the University of Wisconsin, Madison, for the hospitality which I have enjoyed there during my sabbatical leave and which has greatly helped to complete this book. I also thank Fu Jen University, Taipei, for granting the leave.

I am particularly grateful to Todd K. Bender for constructive critical comments on the manuscript and for his encouragement and counsel. Betsy Draine I thank for her interest in my project and for reading the manuscript.

Thanks are due to the British Museum for providing a microfilm of "The Rescuer" manuscript, to the curator of the Albert A. Berg Collection, New York Public Library, and to the personnel of Memorial Library, Madison.

Many thanks go to my friends who in various ways have supported and encouraged me.

ANNOTATION AND ABBREVIATIONS

References to Conrad's works are to the *Collected Works of Joseph Conrad* (London: J.M. Dent, 1946-1955) and to "The Rescuer" (British Museum, Ashley Library, Manuscript 4787). Page references are incorporated into the text. The abbreviations for some much-quoted sources are as follows:

CH Sherry, Norman ed. *Conrad: The Critical Heritage*. London: Routledge & Kegan, 1973.

CL Karl, Frederick R. & Davies, Laurence, ed. *The Collected Letters of Joseph Conrad*. 3 vols. to date. London: Cambridge UP, 1983-.

LL Aubry, G. Jean, ed. *Joseph Conrad: Life and Letters*. 2 vols. New York: Doubleday, 1927.

PR Conrad, Joseph. *A Personal Record*.

A list of works cited other than those given above follows the text at the end of the book.

INTRODUCTION

When with the publication of *Almayer's Folly* Conrad appeared on England's literary horizon, his work immediately attracted an attentive even if limited readership. Conrad was hailed as a literary explorer of a territory hitherto unknown in English fiction. The Malay Archipelago in general and Borneo in particular were a new world for Conrad's readers that held the appeal of the distant and the exotic. They applauded the freshness of the setting and the vividness with which Conrad's imagination presented it.

As the setting had a stimulating effect on his readers, so it had earlier affected the author himself. He returned to it in his second novel, *An Outcast of the Islands*, and again, after a brief attempt at something different, in the third, *The Rescue*. In all three novels he also introduced the character of Captain Lingard whose fame obviously had fascinated Conrad during his engagements in the eastern hemisphere. Thus these novels form a trilogy without having been planned as one. What is more, they establish the pattern on which much of Conrad's work was generated, and they prove that pattern to be analogous to the process at work in the author's life when he left the sea to live by his pen.

In his "Note" to *Lord Jim*, Conrad briefly suggests the nature of that process by speaking of a passing figure, shrouded in a cloud of mystery, which asserted an appeal on his imaginative and creative powers. It was the same mental experience that made him claim that without having met Almayer he would not have become a writer. Not so much Almayer, the idiosyncratic individual, makes the author's protestations sound credible as the Almayer who represents Conrad's contact with the Malay Archipelago. It is probably true in a much more inclusive sense than obvious at first sight or even intended by Conrad. Not only his first novel, but in fact, a great part of his fiction, and among it some of his best works, are the fruit of his sensitivity to the tensions that result from the colonial engagements and imperialistic ambitions of European nations in overseas territories. It was the Malay Archipelago with its truths about human life dimmed by the mists of its jungles and waterways that started Conrad on his career as a novelist.

Those two factors—the evolution of Conrad's art and his choice of a setting that introduced the theme of imperialism—have frequently been the causes of critical interest in his first novels. Conrad's development from an amateur to a self-conscious artist is reflected in the correspondence that accompanied his writing of the three novels as well as in the finished products. From his letters it appears that Conrad's literary preoccupations were intensive and sustained even while he still was actively engaged in seafaring. Writing to Edward Noble in October 1895, he states that there was not a day during the three years in which he was trying to finish *Almayer's Folly* that he did not think of his novel (CL I 252).

The literary theory presented in that letter proves that Conrad devoted much thought to the techniques of novel writing and that in conception he already had evolved the essence of his fictional art while he still was groping for a way to express it. Imagination, he tells his young correspondent, "should be used to create human souls; to disclose human hearts—and not to create events that are properly speaking *accidents* only." This insight was the fruit of careful reading and of close study, especially of French authors. It could hardly have been attained during the brief time since Conrad's last engagement as a sailor which had ended in January 1894.

Conrad's correspondence also suggests that *Almayer's Folly* was begun for the joy of writing, without the tortures caused by self-consciousness and the doubts that accompanied the composition of his following works. It is narrow in scope but richer in content than it might appear at a first reading. For an initial attempt at novel writing it is remarkably well structured and it conveys to the reader an impression of balance and control. Even so, when Conrad thought of its publication, he became conscious of the potential difficulty its narrative device, especially its many time shifts, could hold for the average reader. Was the story clear enough? he asked when he exposed the manuscript to criticism for the first time (PR 17). Before long, he had to realize that his apprehensions were well founded. In spite of the good reviews it received, the novel did not sell.

In writing the second novel, Conrad was conscious of the question of the public's taste which had been raised at his first meeting with T. Fisher Unwin (CL I 180). He had started it in August 1895 while he was waiting for the publisher's response to his first novel. This fact seems interesting since in its preface Conrad credits Edward Garnett, whom he had met only later, with having stimulated its writing. On various occasions he likewise created the impression that he embarked on a writer's career as the result of circumstances and through the urging of others more than by his own decision.

Although Conrad progressed comparatively quickly in writing his second novel, he was subject to distressing uncertainties throughout its composition. He was not yet ready for the lonely path Edward Garnett marked out to him with the advice to "disregard the public's taste" (Garnett 9). Neither was he able to adopt a voice that could reach the masses without impairing his art.

The territory Conrad covers in *An Outcast* is wider and his exploration of the intricacies of human nature is more ambitious than in *Almayer's Folly*. But to most readers this does not justify the close to double length of the novel. The more Conrad attempted to stimulate by vividness the less he achieved his goal. An *Outcast of the Islands* was called wordy, nebulous, diffuse. Like *Almayer's Folly* it had a limited readership.

The next novel was to become Conrad's most trying piece. He began "The Rescuer: A Tale of Narrow Waters" in April 1896, worked on it sporadically for three years, during which he finished the first three parts and a portion of the fourth, and then put it aside only to complete it in 1919. Thus its composition embraces most of Conrad's writing career. Although it differs from the first two novels, because in extensive revisions Conrad cut much of the original text when he prepared the manuscript for print in his late period, enough is retained of his early characteristics to connect it with his first works; in addition there are the Bornean setting, the theme of imperialism, and the Lingard character which they have in common.

It is evident that Conrad did not plan his Lingard trilogy as one whole. But when he found himself returning to characters and settings with which he had dealt earlier, he did aim at some degree of consistency in the inverted development of the Lingard character. Unknowingly he set the stage for the following two novels by choosing a wide focus for the first one. In *Almayer's Folly* Lingard is shown from a distance, mainly through the mind of Almayer who reminisces on how he came to be a trader in Sambir. The broad scope that is gained thereby presents the Rajah Laut from the most successful period of his career to his uncertain end. In the following novel, he moves closer to the center by being actively involved in the life of the protagonist. The time range covered in this novel is slightly more than fifteen years, from Willems' arrival in the East to the moral and economic decline that follows from the younger man's presence in Lingard's life. In the third novel, the focus is on Lingard as the main character, and the time range is the short period covered by the action of the story which, together with the retrospect narrative, does not exceed three years.

In each of the three novels, Lingard is seen from a different angle and invested with a growing amount of responsibility. In both *Almayer's Folly* and *An Outcast* his significance rests on his relation to the younger protagonist as an older benefactor. But whereas in the former his image is drawn by Almayer's subjective memory, Lingard's presence in the latter allows the reader to see and appraise him objectively. To the protagonist of *Almayer's Folly*, Lingard's past involvement in his life is a means by which, early in the novel, he explains and excuses his own present ineffectualness. In *An Outcast*, Captain Lingard's personality and the decisions he makes introduce the important themes of isolation and justice, in addition to those of imperialism and commercial rivalry, and thereby he is of as much consequence in the novel as the protagonist himself. *The Rescue*, finally, centering on Lingard as its protagonist and central force of action shows him as the bearer of all responsibility and of a double duty which, according to his understanding, circumstances and his origin impose on him. The complexity of the situation in which Lingard sees himself caught and the choices he makes in coping with it prove the author's penetration to the intricate nature of these issues and his rejection of simple solutions to the problems that derive from them.

The ironic picture that emerges from Lingard's involvement in the three novels gains in color by the presence of some of the minor characters of *Almayer's Folly* also in *An Outcast*. For a study of the women in these novels, however, attention to transtextual characterization bears little fruit. Only Nina Almayer and her mother figure in more than one novel and, since Nina is her father's foil in *Almayer's Folly* but only an infant in *An Outcast*, little can be gained from her repeated presence. Her mother likewise is insignificant in the latter novel, as she is seen but briefly and exclusively through her husband's eyes.

Nevertheless, the presentations of female characters in the three novels complement each other significantly. When studied with the sequels in mind, trends common to all of them become noticeable. The first of these is the absence of important roles for female characters from the original conceptions of *Almayer's Folly* and *An Outcast*. Only when he revised his first novel, did Conrad introduce the element of paternal love in Almayer's relation to his daughter in the first chapter, as J.D. Gordan has pointed out, and thereby assign to her the role she now plays in the novel. The original title of *An Outcast*, "Two Vagabonds," likewise shows—and the author's letter to Mme Poradowska (Aug. 18, 1894) confirms—that this fiction was to be the story of two male characters. Even Edith Travers in *The Rescue* was intended only as an instrument to cause Lingard's temporary folly, as his letter to Mr. Blackwood (Sept. 6, 1897) makes clear. The timing of the changes by which the author introduced Nina as her father's foil in the first and Willems' women in the second novel and the reasons for these changes are closely connected with his advance from an amateur to a professional literary artist. Thus the roles of the women have to be viewed from this aspect which is closely connected with Conrad's awakening to the fact of reader expectations and his attempt to respond to them.

Setting and themes of these novels, however, add an even more significant aspect to the study of female characters, because they induce Conrad to pair the women who confront the protagonists. In each novel a native female is seen apropos of a half-caste or white woman: Nina with her mother, daughter of Sulu pirates, in *Almayer's Folly*, Joanna with Aïssa in *An Outcast*, Edith Travers with Immada in *The Rescue*. By their differences and similarities, fears and hopes, antagonisms and mutual attractions, frustrations and successes, added to their varying roles in the lives of the protagonists, the author puts forth his views on the systems of which they are a part, be they social, political, economic or cultural.

There is an obvious incongruity between the subordinate roles assigned to these women in the plan of the author and the determination with which they pursue their interests, and by which in consequence they are foils to the protagonists. It corresponds with the author's paradoxical view of the role of women in public life, narrated by Ford Madox Ford, according to which Conrad denied women the right to vote while he admitted that women kept alive the national feeling of Poland when the revolution of 1862 had failed (54). The sense of ambiguity with which the reader is left as to the author's actual intention with those women prompts the question whether it should be seen in connection with his ambiguous relationship with Mme Poradowska and the degree to which she had influenced his choice of writing as a career.

That lady, the widow of a distant relative, was the daughter of a French historian and nine years older than Conrad. With her Polish husband she had spent some time in his native country before settling down in

Belgium. Her literary engagements, which consisted in fiction writing with Polish motifs and translations from that language into French, were well known to Conrad's uncle Bobrowski, who was outspoken in his disapproval of Conrad's relationship with her. He called it flirtation and warned Conrad of the consequences of imprudence. Bobrowski could not fail to realize the woman's potential for influencing his nephew in the direction of the literary occupation which she herself practiced; this seems to have been the stronger reason for his objection.

Bobrowski's apprehensions were justified. *Almayer's Folly* was begun before this friendship was born, but it was continued and completed with the encouragement that Conrad derived from the lady's interest in his work. Mme Poradowska had won for herself a reputation by her publications in the *Revue des Mondes*. She read Conrad's manuscript and nourished his interest in creative writing by sending him her publications. Conrad further developed his capacity for critical analysis and sharpened his sensitivity to matters of style and diction in response to her stimulation.

The significance of this literary interchange for Conrad's turn from sea captain to novelist probably can not be overrated. When during the trying period of waiting for the publisher's response to the manuscript of *Almayer's Folly* he began to doubt whether it would be accepted in England, he was ready to lean on this friendship in order to enter the literary world of France. In August 1895, he suggested to Mme Poradowska that they publish the novel not as a translation in French—which she had agreed to prepare—but as a collaboration. By being mentioned as her junior collaborator, Conrad hoped to gain from her reputation in order to establish himself as a writer (CL I 170).

The essential feature of this episode in Conrad's life—the formative effect of a woman's involvement—is recognizeable also in the novel that shows Lingard as a still unfinished personality. The protagonist of *The Rescue* hardly resembles the character of the same name in the previous novels. His unseamanlike appearance and carriage and his romantic inefficiency in a crisis do not suggest the resourceful trader, the Rajah Laut, of *Almayer's Folly* and *An Outcast of the Islands*. It is by the doubtful role of Edith Travers in *The Rescue* and the "temporary foolishness" through which Lingard passes on account of her presence that he awakens to a corrected comprehension of the realities of his life. As he picks up its fragments at the grave of Jaffir, and in doing so renounces the passions that have incapacitated him in the past, his personality opens up to new possibilities. That Conrad's intention as to the ending of the novel was less pessimistic than seen by most critics is suggested by his letter to his agent Pinker on Feb. 15, 1919, in which he expresses the confidence that this novel might qualify him to be awarded the Nobel Prize (Berg).

This fact brings into focus the tension between Lingard's claims and the destiny which the author assigns to his native friends in *The Rescue*, because it reminds the reader of the novel's title. It is highly ironic not only seen from the perspective of the colonial situation but also from that of the protagonist's future, for which he is rescued from the power of Edith Travers over him. But that effect can be appreciated only if Lingard's career in the two novels that present his later life is kept in mind.

Whether seen in relation to each other or individually, the characters of the Lingard trilogy are highly functional in Conrad's presentation of his ideas on European imperialism. His interest in this phenomenon probably originated in his childhood readings and experiences as much as in his sea journeys that brought him face to face with it in South America, Southeast Asia, and Africa. Avron Fleishman has pointed out that Conrad himself originated in a colonial setting inasmuch as, in the Polish Ukraine, where he was born, the drastic minority of three percent Poles owned most of the land (4). His colonial background made Conrad distinguish between conquerors and colonists, Fleishman concludes, and disposed him to believe in a workable form of colonialism.

Fleishman's observation raises the double question of what, first of all, is meant when we speak of imperialism in Conrad's novels and, secondly, what is the total picture of the author's view of it that emerges from the study of the three Malay novels. A clarification of the term 'imperialism' appears desirable mainly because in applying it, Marxist tendencies in Conrad criticism distinguish little between western capitalism as a system and the relation of that system to underdeveloped countries. Within the frame of this study 'imperialism' refers to the set of values, the sense of mission and racial consciousness that impel Western nations and their individual representatives to seek relationships with other continents which—intentionally or not—in all cases become relations of power and dominance.

Conrad was early prepared to identify such tendencies and to evaluate them later in his fiction. For, the reverse side of his awareness that he derived from colonists was that of having been born into homelessness due to Russia's occupation of the Ukraine. "Baby son, tell yourself / You are without land, without love, / Without country, without people, / While *Poland—your Mother* is entombed," his father wrote at Conrad's birth (Najder 11-12). Corresponding with these lines is Conrad's observation that his childhood memories began in the courtyard of the Warsaw Citadel, where his father was imprisoned after the 1861 insurrection (CL I 358). The following years spent in exile with his parents and their early death could only increase his sense of being "without country, without people."

In consequence, he made the world his homeland by sailing its seas. His reading had acquainted him with England's leading position among maritime and colonial powers. His claim that from the beginning his thought had turned to England, when he had set his heart on leaving Poland, is therefore credible. English trading relations were extensive enough to satisfy Conrad's yearning for adventure, but work on board ship was also sufficiently demanding to have a sobering effect on the young man. In the course of the years, he came to understand not only the unreliability of the glamor of adventure, but also the basically destructive nature of European imperialism which had fascinated him as a youth. He was too much formed by the traditional values of his Polish heritage not to be sensitive to their loss in consequence of the greedy aspirations of western expansionism. He likewise was conditioned by his early experiences of injustice and oppression to recognize them in their various manifestations in human lives, be they caused by Europeans or the natives of colonial territories.

In the Lingard trilogy Conrad comments on imperialism in the eastern hemisphere even though his actual contacts with the setting of these novels were few and brief. His biographers tell us that Conrad left Amsterdam for Samarang on the *Highland Forest*, a merchant sailing vessel, in February 1887. During the voyage he suffered a back injury in a gale and was hospitalized in Singapore for several weeks. After his recovery, in August, he accepted a berth on the *Vidar* which made regular voyages between Singapore, Borneo and Celebes. J.D. Gordan considers the acceptance of this—compared with oversea voyages—easy berth as a consequence of the accident Conrad had suffered (23). But it is equally plausible that his boyhood reading had made Conrad desirous of a closer acquaintance with the Malay Archipelago in the same way as later it affected his acceptance of an assignment on the Congo. In his *Notes on Life and Letters*, Conrad speaks of F.S. Marryat, whose book *Borneo and the Indian Archipelago* had been published in 1848, as an "enslaver of youth" (53). It is a suggestive remark as to the influence that the author had exerted on Conrad himself.

On the *Vidar* Conrad undertook four voyages, each of which lasted from seventeen to thirty-five days. In December of the same year, he resigned his berth with the intention of returning to Europe.

Unexpectedly, however, he was offered the command of the barque *Otago*—his first command. The voyages as master of that ship took him from Bangkok to Australia and Mauritius before, in May 1889, he arrived again in England (Najder 94-113). In the fall of the same year, he started to write what was to become his first novel, *Almayer's Folly*.

To a great extent it was through the efforts of Norman Sherry and Hans van Marle, in addition to Professor Gordan's ground-breaking work, that some of the facts have been brought to light that underlie the settings and characters of Conrad's Malay novels. The *Vidar* was a small steamer commanded by an Englishman, Captain James Craig; it sailed under the British flag, was owned by an Arab merchant in Singapore and called on the out-of-the-way ports between Singapore and Berau. The latter, on the river of the same name, became the Sambir of *Almayer's Folly* and *An Outcast of the Islands* (Sherry 80, 107-117).

Conrad's voyages on the *Vidar* acquainted him with the reputation of Captain William Lingard, the model upon which he shaped his Tom Lingard. Early reviewers of Conrad's first two novels regretted that the author had used the name of a person whom they thought worthy of respect and who had been known in the Malay Archipelago for many years. They felt that Conrad's fictional representation of Lingard was a "libel" on the memory of the real person (Curreli 167). From this Hans van Marle drew the conclusion that Conrad's Tom Lingard was "an easily recognizable figure for old hands in Singapore," and that "the real Captain William Lingard was a highly interesting figure in its own, non-fictional right" (162).

According to Norman Sherry, William Lingard established trading posts at Berau and Bulungan. He became the guardian of the two natural children of a wealthy white trader and a native woman when their father had died. On account of successful fights against pirates of that region, he earned the title "Rajah Laut" by which he named one of his ships. He also surveyed the wide meandering delta of the Berau river and thereby contributed to navigation in its estuary. In his later years Lingard's wealth declined, and, at Conrad's time, the place and circumstances of his death were unknown (89-126). Hans van Marle has solved the mystery of Lingard's end by locating his death certificate at the General Register Office, London, which states that Lingard died at Macclesfield in 1888 (Watts 137).

William Lingard was closely connected with the Olmeijer family who lived in Sourabaya (Gordan 37). His wife was a Miss Johanna Carolina Olmeijer and William Charles Olmeijer, her brother, the Kaspar Almayer of Conrad's first two novels, was one of the protégés whom Lingard established in Berau (Sherry 94-97). According to his daughter Johanna Elizabeth, whom Professor Gordan came to know as Mrs Andrew Gray of Malang, Java, William Charles Olmeijer shared trading interests in guttah, rattan and rubber with Lingard (38). In 1890 he petitioned the Governor- General of the Dutch East Indies for the permission to prospect for gold in Berau (Watts 137). Olmeijer had eleven children and died after a cancer operation in Sourabya in 1900 (Gordan 38).

Another protégé was Jim Lingard, one of his two grand-nephews, whom Lingard had brought to the East and who figures in *An Outcast of the Islands* as Peter Willems (Sherry 99-100). Rivalry among these protégés was a most likely thing to happen and is reflected in the Almayer-Willems relationship in *Almayer's Folly* and *An Outcast*. Cut off from their own civilization, the white traders in the small, retired places in which the *Vidar* called tended to seek company in alcohol or turned into cranks. In *The Sea Years of Joseph Conrad*, Jerry Allen names four such individuals as living in Berau at the time of Conrad's voyages in that region (216-30).

In addition to these main characters, Conrad derived the suggestion for several minor, not less vivid ones, from his experience with the *Vidar*. Babalatchi, Lakamba, Dain Maroola, Abdulla, Reshid, Jim-Eng, Hudig, Ford, and Patalolo are among those whom Professor Gordan has traced to real life characters (46-49). They illustrate how, in writing his first novels, Conrad drew freely from the materials with which his involvement in that part of the world had provided him.

It has been argued that Conrad chose Borneo as the setting of his novels in order to avoid writing about places that were better known to his readers than to himself (Najder 100-1). Although this was a reality worthy of the author's consideration, it is more likely that besides his personal experiences, it was the writings of Frank S. Marryat and James Brooke that decided Conrad's choice. From them he derived a variety of motifs and episodes, and they stimulated his creative imagination, as did the Archipelago's colonial history, the traces of which were very much visible even at Conrad's time. He refers to it directly in the opening of *The Rescue* mentioning Portugal, Spain, England, and Holland, who through past centuries had contested for supremacy in the region.

Glimpses of a history of Borneo show archeological finds of a relatively highly developed stone age culture and evidence of Dyak trade relations with the Chinese and Siamese as early as the tenth century A.D. Trade engagements and settlers from other parts of the Archipelago made Islam spread in the coastal regions during the two hundred years preceding the arrival of the Europeans in the early sixteenth century.

Meanwhile, the Dyak in the interior of the island remained nearly untouched by these influences.

With the coming of western colonizers, a prolonged period of rivalry began that ended only in the nineteenth century with the final carving up of the territory among the most prominent powers—the English and the Dutch. The Portuguese were the first on the scene. They established themselves in Malacca, which flourished in spice trade, and from 1530 Brunei, on the north-west coast of Borneo, was commercially tied to that Portuguese stronghold. From 'Brunei' the island derived the name 'Borneo' among westerners while in Indonesian it retained the original 'Kalimantan'. The presence of the Portuguese did not keep the Spanish, who had established themselves in the Philippines, from launching forays on Brunei, especially in 1578. But neither the Portuguese nor the Spanish succeeded in asserting themselves permanently, and finally both yielded to the stronger claims of the Dutch and the English.

The former arrived in the Archipelago toward the end of the sixteenth century and established the Dutch East India Company. For two centuries their competitor was the English East India Company. On account of the widening of political and economic involvements in the nineteenth century, however, English interests gradually concentrated on the northern part of the island as a strategic point of its trade route between India and China. In a similar way, the Dutch, whose colonial government was based in Java, concentrated their interests on southern Borneo (Ave and King 14-22). Thus it was the advance of industrial capitalism in Europe and the resulting need for raw materials, expanding markets, as well as new outlets for investment that drew Borneo into the current of a development that brought about the breaking up of earlier structures. During his brief sojourn in the East, Conrad became witness to these developments and registered them in his Malay novels.

Over the years each of them has received a fair amount of critical attention. Frequently, the contradictory claims and ambitions of the colonists, the transformations which Europeans underwent in colonial settings, and the consequences of colonialization for the local population have engaged the critics' minds just as they had stimulated the author. Among the evaluations of Conrad's fiction from these aspects in the last decade, John A. McClure, *Kipling & Conrad: The Colonial Fiction* (Cambridge, Mass.: Harvard UP, 1981) and Hunt Hawkins "Conrad and the Psychology of Colonialism" in *Conrad Revisited: Essays for the Eighties* ed. Ross C. Murfin (Alabama: Alabama UP, 1985) are significant.

McClure's analysis resumes the direction taken by E.K. Hay and Avron Fleishman, according to whose studies in the sixties the Lingard novels lead to a recognition of Conrad's anti-imperialism. McClure finds in them a demystification of the colonial past and the dramatization of a law by which the inequities of European civilization are visited upon those whom its representatives claim to colonize. H. Hawkins' essay furnishes the psychological basis of such a reading inasmuch as he explains the assumptions underlying the colonists' mode of conduct and the natives' response to it. Benita Parry, *Conrad and Imperialism: Ideological Boundaries and Visionary Frontiers* (London: Macmillan, 1983) likewise exposes Conrad's refutation of the colonial myth in *The Rescue*. But she dismisses his concern with this issue in the first two novels as "relatively simplistic," whereby she excludes the possibility to view characters in perspective.

Daniel R. Schwarz, *Conrad: Almayer's Folly to Under Western Eyes* (Ithaca, N.Y.: Cornell UP, 1980) and *Conrad: The Later Fiction* (London: Macmillan, 1982) follow the line of Bernard Meyer's psychoanalytical biography inasmuch as both take Conrad's saying that "a novelist lives in his work" as the guiding line for their approach to his life and work. Schwarz finds in the first two Malay novels a reflection of the author's search for identity and in *The Rescue* narcissistic implications of his preoccupation with redeeming it. *The Rescue* is also given much attention in Gary Geddes, *Conrad's Later Novels* (Montreal: McGill-Queens UP, 1980), and it is the object of Robert Caserio's essay "*The Rescue* and the Ring of Meaning" in *Conrad Revisited*. Both are concerned with Conrad's art in this novel. Geddes suggests that it can be read as a "tragedy of manners" in which the author explores the relation between the psychology of his characters and the sense appeals they create by their manners. It was this attempt of the author, Geddes reasons, that resulted in Conrad's prolonged search for the right mode of expression. Caserio's analysis digs deeper. He discusses the modes of representation which Conrad employs in *The Rescue* to prove the representational nature and value of his novels as a "union of romance with the discovery of truth."

The most comprehensive recent study of the first Lingard novel is a chapter in Ian Watt, *Conrad in the Nineteenth Century* (Berkeley: U of California P, 1979). Like Parry's important contribution, however, it does not trace relations to the two sequels to the novel, an approach recommended as greatly rewarding in Cedric Watts, *The Deceptive Text: An Introduction to Covert Plots* (Brighton: The Harvester P, 1984). In light of the insights this study has brought to the understanding of the

Malay novels by pointing out the gain from attention to transtextual characterization, this informal trilogy calls for a study that focuses on the novels from the larger perspectives of all three. In this way, more comprehensive outlines can be gained not only as regards the quality of Conrad's early fictional art, which parts of *The Rescue* have in common with *Almayer's Folly* and *An Outcast of the Islands*, but also with respect to thematic preoccupations. A look at the novels in relation to each other should put into clearer light issues common to all of them.

Conrad's Lingard Trilogy

ALMAYER'S FOLLY

I FICTION WRITING AS PASTIME

Much of 1889, the year in which Captain Konrad Korzenjowski began to write his first novel, found him relatively inactive in London. While he was trying to find a command of a ship, he started preparations to visit his uncle Bobrowski in the Ukraine. With his release from the status of Russian subject in March, a return to the places of his earliest childhood, without the danger of being drafted by the Russians, had moved within the realm of possibilities.

Neither a new command offered itself quickly, however, nor was the visa for a journey to Poland easily obtained. These were trying experiences for Conrad. In *A Personal Record* he speaks of the circumstance that gave birth to his first novel as "idleness" rather than "leisure" (68). "The conception of a planned book was entirely outside my mental range when I sat down to write; . . ." But he acknowledged the significance of that seemingly unpremeditated action saying, "yet it stands clear as the sun at noonday that from the moment I had done blackening over the first manuscript page of 'Almayer's Folly' . . . from the moment I had in the simplicity of my heart and the amazing ignorance of my mind, written that page the die was cast" (68-9). Whether these lines, written two decades later, faithfully express his sensations of that time or not, it remains a fact that in the autumn of 1889 Captain Konrad Korzeniowski took his first steps towards his career as a novelist. According to Zdzislaw Najder, Conrad may have finished the first three chapters before he started on his journey to Poland in January 1890 (117).

In *A Personal Record*, Conrad speaks of one visit "to the scenes . . . of [his] childhood" while writing *Almayer's Folly* (13). His remark that he had started the ninth chapter by that time suggests that Conrad thought of his visit to the Ukraine in the summer of 1893, when he nearly lost the manuscript in a Berlin railway station (19). But, as it often happened when the author recalled events of the past, his memory was not fully reliable. It fused events of his visit to the Ukraine in 1890 with those of the later one. This is obvious from a letter he quotes in which his uncle informs Conrad that he would be met at the railway station in Kalinowka with a small sledge (20). Later he mentions that the writing table in the guest room, on which he placed the manuscript of *Almayer's Folly*, had been awaiting "the son of the favorite sister" for "some fifteen years or so" (22). Both passages are evidence that the author was referring to his visit to Poland in the early months of 1890.

There is a revealing slip in a letter written in March of that year which betrays Conrad's preoccupation with his novel while in Kazimierowska. "Probably he is living in Sambir, but I do not know how he is getting on," he wrote about his former tutor Adam Pulman, who for some time was living in Sambor, Galicia (CL I 45). The conclusion is that the manuscript of *Almayer's Folly* was with Conrad on both journeys to Poland.

It certainly accompanied him up the Congo river to the region of the Stanley Falls in 1890. With the habitual need for playing down the importance his writing had for him, Conrad speaks of the "special dispensation of Providence" that preserved the manuscript among his luggage while other "infinitely more valuable" items got lost on the way (PR 14). It returned with him to London in January 1891 and in May, when he had sufficiently recovered from the illness that had necessitated his return to Europe to take up writing again, the manuscript had grown to six chapters. In the Swiss spa Champel-les-Baines on the outskirts of Geneva, he began to write the seventh (Najder 147).

On November 16 of that year Conrad accepted the position of first mate on the passenger clipper *Torrens*, and two days later he left for Australia. During the course of the following two years he made two round voyages between London and Adelaide, the second of which is memorable as regards Conrad's occupation with *Almayer's Folly*. During that voyage, begun on October 25, 1892, Conrad for the first time exposed the still unfinished manuscript to the critical evaluation of a reader. The person who had gained his confidence by his calm, unassuming conduct was William Henry Jacques, a Cambridge student, who suffered from consumption and travelled for his health. Was the story "intelligible in its action?" was it "worth finishing?"—these were the questions to which Conrad claims to have been given the brief but definite answers, "Yes! Perfectly" and "Distinctly" (PR 17-18).

On the return voyage, Conrad became acquainted with Edward Lancelot Sanderson and John Galsworthy, who travelled from New Zealand and Australia respectively back to England. The latter had recently qualified himself as a lawyer; he still was distant from his later literary occupations. But the acquaintance was to develop into a friendship which was no less intact when Galsworthy established himself as a novelist. Conrad's relation with the Sandersons likewise became a lasting one. In the following years, while he completed the last chapters of *Almayer's Folly*, and while he expected its publication, he repeatedly spent some days with the Sandersons in Elstree, Hertfordshire (CL I 152, 206). These acquaintances were like an omen. For, when the *Torrens* arrived in London on July 26, 1893, Conrad had, without being aware of it, finished his last long-distance voyage.

In the summer Conrad paid another visit to his uncle Bobrowski in the Ukraine, during which he worked on chapter nine of his novel, as has been shown earlier. After his return to England, in November 1893, he tried himself once more at the seafaring life by accepting a berth as second mate on the steamship *Adowa*. This steamer was intended to carry emigrants from France to Canada. For some reason, however, the planned voyage did not take place; the *Adowa* and her crew lay idle in the port of Rouen and then returned to London (PR 3-6). With the ship's arrival there on January 17, 1894, Conrad's service at sea came to an end. He may not have recognized the historical significance of the moment when he signed off from the *Adowa*. But neither was he quite unaware that in doing so a new stage of his life was beginning. For it was the first time that he signed his name in the way by which he was to become famous as an author—Joseph Conrad (Certificate of Discharge, *Adowa*).

A month later, Conrad received the news of the sudden death of his uncle. The pain this loss caused him was deep and genuine, as a brief note to Mme Poradowska suggests. "It seems as if everything has died in me. He seems to have carried my soul away with him" (CL I 148). For his embarkation on his new career, however, the event had a favorable effect. Probably on account of the temporary relief from financial worries which his expected inheritance was to bring him, Conrad was able to concentrate on the completion of his novel. In March he struggled with chapter eleven (CL I 152); then he immediately continued to work on the final chapter, and on April 24 he informed Mme Poradowska, "I regret to inform you of the death of Mr Kaspar Almayer, which occurred this morning at 3 o'clock" (CL I 153).

The first draft was finished; it was in need of a revision, however, which seems to have been more difficult for Conrad than its composition. "I find the job of revising my first three chapters not only disagreeable but absolutely painful. And difficult as well! And yet it must be done," he wrote to Mme Poradowska on May 2, 1894 (CL I 156). The changes which Conrad made introduced the element of paternal affection in Almayer's conversation with his daughter in the first chapter and the change affected the novel essentially.

By the middle of May, the work of revision seems to have been completed. "Forgive me for not sending you my Chapter XII," he wrote on May 17, "the whole manuscript is in the hands of a rather distinguished critic, Edmund Gosse" (CL I 158). Zdzislaw Najder expresses doubts whether this communication was based on facts; he prefers to consider it an expression of wishful thinking (168). Another explanation could be that Conrad was anxious to submit the manuscript to a publisher and therefore did not wish to send the final chapter to Belgium, as he had promised earlier. The reason he gave would have been a convenient excuse.

Whatever the fact may have been, the typescript of *Almayer's Folly* was sent to the publishing house of T. Fisher Unwin on July 4, 1894. It was

> enclosed in brown paper wrapper addressed to J. Conrad. 17 Gillingham St S.W. and franked for return by parcel post, by twelve 1^d stamps. The brown paper package was put between *two* detached sheets of cardboard secured together by a string. One of the cardboard sheets bore Your address.

This is the communication which the author sent to the publisher on September 8, 1894. He had been anxiously waiting for a response for two full months. When he could no longer bear the uncertainty, he expressed the hope that the manuscript be returned to him if it was not considered good enough for publication (CL I 172-3). On October 2 he wrote, "I cannot get hold of my manuscript. I have asked twice, and each time I have been told that they are attending to it" (CL I 175).

Earlier, in July, he had proposed to Mme Poradowska to publish *Almayer's Folly* in French "not as a translation but as a collaboration" (CL I 165). He had assumed the pseudonym "Kamudi" in the typescript of *Almayer's Folly* in order to have the novel included in Unwin's Pseudonym Library (Najder 531n94). This name he wanted to use in the French edition of the novel as well; it was "a Malay word meaning rudder," he explained (CL I 170).

Finally, on October 3, a letter from T. Fisher Unwin brought the good news that the novel was accepted for publication. In his reply on the following day, Conrad expressed unwillingness to part with the copyright for £20 and mentioned the arrangements for a translation into French which he had made. "Now I should like immensely to appear in the 'Revue' and still more to have the advantage of being translated by such a competent and charming writer. I trust You will see no objection in Mme Poradowska carrying out her plan" (CL I 176). A few days later he was able to write to that lady, "Victory. I have the French copyright for myself alone" (CL I 180).

One of the two readers whom Conrad mentions in the following line was Wilfrid Hugh Chesson (1870-1952). Edward Garnett (1868-1937), another of Unwin's readers, states that he met Conrad for the first time in November (Garnett 2). Chesson was the first to evaluate Conrad's manuscript. With his favorable comments he passed it on to Garnett who then agreed that the novel was worth publishing. Thus Chesson can justly be called the "discoverer" of Joseph Conrad (Najder 170). But it was Edward Garnett with whom the author established a lasting friendship, who accompanied Conrad's literary career with sincere interest, assisted him in his ups and downs with his sound advice and encouragements, and patiently bore with his foibles and idiosyncrasies.

Very soon Conrad was in need of such a friend. He was suffering from depression and doubted the value of his literary achievement. "I have already thought, on several occasions," he wrote in November 1894 to his favorite correspondent of that time, "that you were doing yourself an injustice in offering to translate *Almayer.* . . . No doubt they will send you the advance sheets, but I beg you to put them aside" (CL I 184). Poradowska was preoccupied with a novel she was writing; nothing came of Conrad's arrangement with her, and in March of the following year, he informed his publisher that she was too unwell to undertake the task. At the same time, he expressed the hope that Mr. Unwin would assist him in negotiating a French translation of *Almayer's Folly.* Only in 1919 did Conrad's dream to see the novel published in French come true (CL I 203n5).

On Christmas Eve 1894, the first proofs of *Almayer's Folly* arrived. "I was horrified," he writes, "absolutely horrified by the thing in print, looking so stupid—worse—senseless" (CL I 193). The proofreading did not cheer him up; nor did the prospect that Chesson, who was entrusted with the task of setting Conrad's novel in print, would handle it "very tenderly" (CL I 197). While he expressed contentment with being in Chesson's hands, he was hunted by latent doubts and misgivings. He had just written a preface to his novel in which he had expressed important views on the theme of imperialism which he treats in the novel. Probably in the hope of receiving a reassuring answer, he remarked, "I trust it may be dispensed with" (CL I 199). Chesson did not know the author well enough to understand what later Edward Garnett was able to observe about him: "When Conrad was particularly pleased with his work he pooh-poohed it in his letters" (Garnett 27). He complied with what he must have taken for the author's wish and did not include it. Only in the *Collected Edition* of 1921 was the "Author's Note" finally published (CL I 199n2).

Neither the publisher nor the author himself could have foreseen the far-reaching consequences of that omission. Even in his advanced age Conrad still felt misunderstood by his readers and critics who placed his Malay fiction besides Stevenson's and Kipling's and expressed dissatisfaction, because it did not meet their expectations of adventure stories. The author's choice of legal terms and court room imagery in writing the preface insinuates that the novel wants to make the reader see facts in order to form a correct and just judgment. He is concerned, Conrad assures his reader, with the facts of life behind exotic and romantic appearances; he exposes the basic sameness of humankind in civilized and uncivilized countries, and aims at a self-identification of the reader with members of the human species in the distant parts of the world. General awareness of the beliefs which Conrad expressed in those lines might have spared him and his readers many frustrating experiences and saved him from the suspicion of racist tendencies.

In the same letter to Chesson, Conrad expressed the hope that in the "literary notices of the publication" *Almayer's Folly* be introduced as a "civilized story in savage surroundings" (CL I 199). The following unsigned notice was printed in the *Daily News* on April 25, four days before the publication of the novel:

> No novelist has yet annexed the island of Borneo—in itself almost a continent. But Mr. Joseph Conrad, a new writer, is about to make the attempt in a novel entitled *Almayer's Folly*, which Mr. Unwin will publish. Mr. Conrad says that he combines 'the psychological study of a sensitive European living alone among semi-hostile Arabs and Malays with the vivid incidents attaching to the life of pirates and smugglers.' A merely 'sensitive' European has no business among the semi-savages of Borneo. What you want is an unbounded, reckless hospitality to all sorts of impressions. However the story is

praised by those who have seen it in manuscript. The author is intimately acquainted with Borneo and its people. The physical setting of his story is as picturesque as the world offers. The European's closest friend is an ex-pirate, and the reassertion of the old savage instinct in the pirate's lovely daughter—an atavistic fit, if that be not too rude an expression—is one of the chief incidents of the tale. The book is to be included in Mr. Unwin's Library of Six Shilling Fiction. (CH 47)

At Conrad's first meeting with Mr. Unwin and the two readers, he was told that they planned to publish his novel in April of the following year. Since that was the season for new publications, they were rather certain that due notice would be taken of the novel in literary journals. But Conrad's chronically difficult financial situation, coupled with uncertainty, made him impatient for an earlier date of publication. In February he wrote, "*Almayer* will be published the first week in March" (CL I 202). On the twelfth of that month he asked Mr. Unwin, "Isn't the 18th the date for the appearance of a certain Immortal work?!" (CL I 204). But another six weeks were to pass before the novel did come out. The time of waiting was a trial for the author till finally, on April 29, 1895, after five years of intermittent work, *Almayer's Folly* was published.

Its reception ranged from enthusiastic welcome to harsh rejection. "Altogether the book is as dull as it well could be," an anonymous reviewer wrote in the *World* (CH 51). But positive criticism outweighed the negative comments. The novelty of the setting, the power of the imagination that created the story, the forcefulness of its presentation made *Almayer's Folly* a "remarkable book" in the eyes of most reviewers. Repeatedly the hope was expressed that more novels by the same author would follow. Writing for *Saturday Review*, H.G. Wells spoke of *Almayer's Folly* as a "work of art . . . a very powerful story indeed, with effects that will certainly capture the imagination and haunt the memory of the reader. . . . It is indeed exceedingly well imagined and well written, and it will certainly secure Mr. Conrad a high place among contemporary story tellers" (CH 53). The *Daily Chronicle* ended a lengthy, mostly favorable review with a similarly encouraging prediction, "Mr. Conrad may go on, and with confidence; he will find his public, and he deserves his place" (CH 50).

On the author who, as in the previous year, was submitting himself to water treatment in the Swiss spa Champel near Geneva, this reception of his novel had an uplifting effect. He felt flattered: "The entire provincial press has spoken favourably, some enthusiastically, of my *Folly*. A big London newspaper has also spoken in the most pleasant terms." But he remained realistic enough to interpret silences correctly: "Otherwise, the critics are keeping me waiting. There are evidently those who hesitate to make any decision, but straws tossed into the wind are floating in the right direction" (CL I 221).

Captain Korzeniowski had successfully introduced himself into the literary world. The future had to show whether he would obtain the place that had been prophesied to him. It would put that in the new author to the test which made *Almayer's Folly* much more of a "promise" than a "performance." At present, however, the atmosphere created by the "promise" of *Almayer's Folly* was propitious for Conrad's continued occupation with writing, and thus his change to a new career was definite.

II THE IMPERIAL THEME AS FATHER-DAUGHTER ANTITHESIS

The society into which Conrad places his protagonist in *Almayer's Folly* is a conglomeration of heterogeneous elements made up of Malays and Arabs. As the only white man among them, Almayer is the exponent of all that they admire, despise, and hate in the world which he represents. Despite his practical unimportance, he is of significance as a living reminder of the claims on the territory which the Dutch occasionally assert. By his presence Almayer frustrates the dream of independence in which the leaders of the settlement like to indulge. The activities by which they circumvent and counteract white dominion are as covert as the undercurrents of a stream, and like these they are indefatigable in affecting the developement of the plot.

The rejection which Almayer experiences in Sambir is fully reciprocated by his hatred for the settlement and his sense of superiority over its inhabitants. Thus the novel presents the curious situation of a colonizer trapped by his doubtful scale of values which condemn him to a masochistic form of existence in an isolated colonial territory. The approach Conrad takes to the discussion of European involvement in the Malay Archipelago exposes the weaknesses of the civilization that has produced Almayer through contrasting effects with indigenous life. It is as indirect an approach as the tensions that result from Almayer's unwanted presence in Sambir are covert due to calculating diplomacy. With his presentation of the main character as ineffectual and weak, the author establishes a correlation with the climate and setting, which are enervating and demoralizing. In this way Conrad allows those elements to prove themselves that by their natural conditioning resist the effects of both.

When Almayer awakens from the reverie in which he is absorbed as the novel opens, his attention is caught by an uprooted tree in the river that passes his "new" house. It is only one of many logs that float toward the sea in consequence of previous storms and floods. But Almayer's attention is attracted by this specific tree for the reason that it is "grounded on the shelving shore, just by the house," before the force of the water carries it along. Interest in the tree is built up with its further progress: "The tree swung slowly round, amid the hiss and foam of the water, and soon getting free of the obstruction began to move downstream again, rolling slowly over, raising upwards a long, denuded branch, like a hand lifted in mute appeal to heaven against the river's brutal and unnecessary violence" (4). Due to the envy it arouses in Almayer when finally it has freed itself from the impediments that threaten to obstruct its passage down-river, this inanimate object functions as an important symbol.

Having been recognized as a key image, the drifting log invites speculation as to whom or what it is meant to represent. It clearly does not simply stand for Almayer who remains caught in Sambir to the end of his life, whereas the reader is assured that the tree will reach the sea. If the log is seen as standing for Dain Maroola, who escapes from the Dutch authorities in Sambir, the novel might be read as Dain's story in the first place. This would be a serious misreading, because there can be no doubt that *Almayer's Folly* centers on the character after which it is named. The symbolic function of the floating tree can therefore not be limited to either one of these characters. It has wider, more inclusive implications, which become gradually apparent as the novel develops.

After it has recalled Almayer's mind from his dream of a future in Amsterdam, the drifting log causes him to ponder his past. The reader readily sees that past and future are balanced against each other by the same motivating value—comfort and ease through wealth—and the presence of another person as a determining factor. As Nina is to be instrumental for her father to achieve his dream in the future, so Lingard was to be the means for it in the past.

This, however, is only part of what the narrative tells. There is no tinge of gold on the river at present and the drifting log struggles against the force of the element. Almayer's existence is similarly bleak. Since past and future meet in the present, his view of the former prompts the question how Almayer will meet the challenge of the floating tree in the future, because he clearly sees himself as a victim not of his own miscalculations, but of the person who has triggered them—Tom Lingard. At the same time, the reader recognizes in Almayer's reminiscence a record of two ambitions that were pitted against each other: Lingard's vanity and Almayer's greed.

The initial contention of the white men's hopes and wills explains the presence of Almayer in a setting for which he feels only distaste, his attitude towards the natives and his daughter, and his stubborn nurturing of a dream of future wealth. It functions as a key to the novel, and the significance of Lingard's role is therefore beyond doubt. But since he remains outside the direct action of the novel, the reader has to identify the precise nature of his impact on it by relying on the information which the first chapters provide.

The narrator introduces Lingard in the hierarchical order of his relation to peers, Malays, and subjects. The figure that emerges is a subtle mixture of virtues and vices. Lingard excels other white traders in courage and achievement and also in dissipation; honest fishermen as well as desperate pirates acknowledge him as "King of the Sea," and this suggests an affinity with both. He is generous in giving and providing, but is so with total disregard for the wishes and real needs of the persons whom he thus subjugates. The complexity which is suggested in this way contradicts the repeated claims that Lingard is simple.

A sorting out of epithets and modifiers associated with Lingard's person helps to see him more clearly. Besides being the "Rajah Laut," "King of the Sea," "victorious captain," Lingard is called an "old adventurer," "old seaman," "old seadog," "old trader," "old man"; for Almayer, he invariably is "old Lingard." The repetition of the modifier 'old' is striking. It suggests connotations of familiarity and esteem, but in Almayer's mind, which is preoccupied with the money that he will inherit at Lingard's passing away, it undoubtedly refers to age. With the decision to retire from his career at sea, where he is considered a King, to hunt for treasures in the obscure interior of the island, Lingard affirms this meaning. It is of importance to notice that in *Almayer's Folly* he takes this step with the establishment of the new trading station in Sambir and not, as in the second novel, in consequence of the presence of the Arabs on the Pantai. But the new trading company nevertheless bears Lingard's name; it is Lingard & Co., which means that he entrusts his future as a trader to Almayer, the younger man.

The result is an obvious setting off of 'old' from 'new' and 'young.' But the first mention of Almayer's 'new' house as an already decaying one—later it is called a "new ruin"—and that of his youth as a matter of regret and of a distant past undermine the reader's trust in the surface meaning of these words.

A look at further examples proves that more often than not they are employed to negate themselves or to convey negative meanings. Almayer's "new hopes" for a "new existence" merely mean the revival of very old dreams; the "new life" to which Lingard subjects the daughter of pirates and the "new faith" which is imposed on her are an increase of suffering and superstition rather than newness of life and faith which would entail change and growth; likewise, "new misfortunes" and "new complications" are added rather than unprecedented ones. Only with the arrival of Dain Maroola in Sambir as a "new trader," the element of real newness enters the novel, because it is by his presence that both Nina and Taminah are awakened to a consciousness of their existence that they had never experienced before.

The repetition of the phrase "new existence" in reference to Almayer's stale dreams of a leisurely life in Amsterdam (5), to Nina's first awareness of love as a principle for living (64), and the transient state of Taminah's infatuation (115) illustrates the various connotations of 'new' in this novel most effectively. In contrast to that of Almayer, Nina's vision of a different future conveys a sense of hopefulness, because her ready personality lifts it out of the realm of empty dreams. The best proof for this is the manner in which she brings about her first encounter with Dain Maroola in opposition to the expressed wish of both parents. For Taminah, however, the change from unconsciousness to perception is an awakening to hopelessness, pain, and anger.

Similar to 'new,' 'young' is hardly free from negative implications, except in reference to Nina and Dain. Almayer's reminiscence of his younger years is tainted by the awareness of his advance in age; so are those of Lakamba and Mrs Almayer later in the novel. In relation to Lingard, the mention of the youth of Almayer and his wife implies that it facilitated victimization; in the Dutch sub-lieutenant it is seen as a potential cause for imprudent action. Although at times Nina's youth also suggests her being unformed, it mostly expresses hopefulness and a ready approach toward the unknown. Repeated mention of young vegetation as a frame for the lover's meetings conveys a sense of their harmony with nature and with life, which guarantees renewal and newness following victimization and death.

The frequently paradoxical use of the modifiers 'new' and 'young' echoes the paradox of the decaying "new" house throughout the novel and supports its function as a metaphor. Readers easily recognize Almayer's new construction as an image of the dilapidated state of the trading station in general and of Almayer's condition in particular. If Lingard's role in the novel is considered, however, it becomes obvious that more deep-reaching meanings are intended. For, when the old Captain entrusts Lingard & Co., to young Almayer, he fails to realize that a smaller number of years does not necessarily guarantee greater vigor and application. Nor does he register the fact that his own success in "getting his way" is due to Almayer's lack of will power.

Almayer joins the venture only in expectation of a rich inheritance, which means that his motivation is directed towards the older man's completion of life. Apart from Lingard and his wealth there is no sustaining factor for Almayer's life in Sambir, and when Lingard puts his hope in Almayer, he paradoxically hopes for his own end. Even twenty years later, Almayer still follows this pattern of simultaneous affirmation and denial when he is willing to use a despised Malay, Dain Maroola, and Lingard's notebooks to obtain wealth.

Insofar as Lingard first activates this dubious approach to life, which Almayer has inherited in a predominantly materialistically oriented home, it is therefore justifiable to say that despite the positive qualities which he undoubtedly has, he functions as a principle of negation and disruption in *Almayer's Folly*. For with his first act of pressuring two young people into a life that is hateful to both, he triggers a chain of reactions that reverberate through the novel and affect all aspects of the lives that are involved. The rifles and gunpowder which he trades for the products of the natives are a visible expression of his moral influence.

Significantly, the repercussions also affect Lingard's indirect presence in the novel in the form of a steady diminution of the things by which it is suggested: trade falls away from Lingard & Co. the Company's name on the office door becomes illegible, the wharf rots and the godowns fall into disrepair. When after Nina's departure Almayer burns the house that Lingard has built as the headquarters of his company, the jetty still remains till that also is washed away by a flood.

In the colonial setting of this novel, the role of Captain Lingard is an unmistakable comment on European imperialist ambitions: self-interest renders them suspect even in their most benevolent form and in the end they defeat themselves. Beyond that, it also is a comment on the civilization that has formed Lingard and Almayer, who fail to realize that youth is not necessarily commensurate with vitality, as well as on the Malay and Arab society of the colonial setting, for, Lingard serves only to establish the context in which the main character acts. He is, as it were, part of the element against which the floating tree of the introductory image struggles, and when the narrative turns away from Lingard and the past, Almayer's life is shown alongside that of his half-caste daughter Nina.

By introducing her, Conrad accentuates the imperial theme in the contrasting value systems of East and West, for, being of mixed parentage, the girl unites in her person her father's European background with the indigenous forces against which he struggles when he competes with his wife and Dain Maroola for the love of his daughter. As a potential link between both, she comments on them by the choices she makes. At the same time, her contrastive presence shows up the chances and possibilities that have offered themselves to Almayer in the past and are offering themselves during the three days of the novel's immediate action.

The image of the drifting tree calls to mind the famous passage in *Lord Jim* in which the collector of butterflies, Stein, philosophizes on the human condition: "A man that is born," Stein says, "falls into a dream like a man who falls into the sea. If he tries to climb out into the air as inexperienced people endeavor to do, he drowns . . . The way is to the destructive element submit yourself, and with the exertions of your hands and feet in the water make the deep, deep sea keep you up" (214). These lines have often been taken as a warning against the attempt to escape from the realities of life (the sea) into a dream (the air). But Jim's career and dilemma are closer to A.J. Guerard's interpretation of the passage: "A man is born ready to create an idealized conception of self, an ego-ideal. If he tries to escape or transcend this conception of self, he collapses. He should accept this ideal and try through action to make it 'viable'" (165-6). This reading of the passage is supported by Stein's life, of which we are told that it had humble origins and that it had led to the experience of "all the exalted elements of romance" because of his unwavering consistency in following the dream.

Seen in light of Stein's reflection, the first grounded and then drifting tree stands for both characters in this novel who are preoccupied with dreams, Almayer and his daughter. The question is whether and how their dreams are made viable. The opening chapter shows them as prisoners in Sambir. In the case of Almayer we are told directly that he feels as one. About Nina, the reader is made to understand that there is a world beyond that of her home towards which her heart tends. The first glimpse we catch of her shows her "turned towards the outer darkness," with an expression of "impatient expectancy" (16).

The parallels between father and daughter underline the contrasting developments which their lives take. Both have chosen life in Sambir due to a misapprehension of reality. In his mercenary wedding to Lingard's adopted daughter, Almayer failed to realize that a trading station demanded effort in order to yield profit. Nina's unexpected return from Singapore was based on the illusion that her home in Sambir would offer security and harmony. In both cases disillusionment followed without delay. Almayer found hard work instead of ease, competition and deprivation instead of the wealth he had expected. Nina's discovery was that, instead of peace, her parental home could offer only hatred and strife.

In both cases the dreams by which these two persons attempt to escape from an unloved reality originate in the choice of a mate. Almayer's dream is bound up with the intention to get rid of the girl he marries as a necessary but inconvenient means toward his goal of wealth. Nina accepts the death-in-life existence of her parental home with seeming indifference before the arrival of Dain Maroola. Whatever dreams there may be within her heart remain unacknowledged and undefined. Taminah, the only person in the settlement with whom Nina communicates during that time, is the objectification of her mental condition. Of the slave girl, we are told that she is "seeking the light, desiring the sunshine, fearing the storm, unconscious of either" (112). Only when Dain enters Nina's life, she experiences it consciously; "then I began to live," she says of herself.

With the presence of Dain Maroola among the Almayers, the essential difference between the dreams of father and daughter becomes obvious. From the first moment of their meeting, Nina's attention concentrates on the person of the young trader, that of her father on the purpose of his coming and on the probability of material gains deriving from it. The immediacy of her response engages her whole personality so that she recognizes in Dain the person of her dreams. Almayer remains distant and centered in his mental bubble of ease and wealth; his imagination is unstimulated. Ironically he refers to Nina's appearance in the presence of the visitor as being of "no consequence" and demands an explanation from her for having shown herself to the young trader. What he sees at Dain's departure is a "heap of rubbish and broken bottles at the foot of the verandah," while his daughter's eyes are fixed on the boat that takes away the young man. Her gaze is goal-directed despite the vapors of the river that aim to absorb Dain in the atmosphere of uncertainty which is typical of dreams.

The different responses to Maroola set the pattern of characteristic contrasts between father and daughter. Whereas an analysis of Almayer's vision reveals that he himself is at its center—for, the satisfaction he derives from making Nina the wealthiest woman comes from looking on her as an extension of himself—Nina's being reaches out to Dain. The immediate object of Almayer's concern, the gold of the mountain, is materialistic; its ultimate goal his self-fulfillment. Nina's objectives are the secrets of the heart, and her final aim the triumph of life over death. Nina's scale of values differs radically from that of her father, and the fear that in consequence takes hold of Almayer is a proof that he interprets Nina's passionate character correctly. It also shows most clearly the difference between the daughter's quest for life and the father's life-shunning attitude.

Numerous examples throughout the novel illustrate this basic difference between the white man and his half-caste daughter. On the evening of Dain's return to Sambir, Almayer's exclusive preoccupation is with the chance he has for finding the gold deposits. His regained hope makes him happy. Nina is far from being so. She is apprehensive about the safety of her lover in the camp of Lakamba and in the storm. This intensity of personal engagement keeps her awake and expectant while her father sleeps. The inconsistency of Almayer's claim that all he does is for the good of his daughter is most striking while he prepares for the expedition upriver. He builds castles in the air for Nina, but he is oblivious of her physical presence and ignores Dain, the crutch by which he supports his hope. Meanwhile, Nina's life experiences that invigoration and expansion that derives from the affirmation which comes with love, given and received, even though it still is in the initial stage of mainly physical appeal.

Her relations to Dain are not at all free from self-seeking considerations. Like her father, who has plans for her greatness, she finds satisfaction in thinking of the future greatness which she will bring about for her lover: "She was thinking already of moulding a god from the clay at her feet" (172). The difference between her ambitions and those of her father is that in Nina's plan she is the moving force for Dain's achievements through the love by which she means to urge him on. The readiness for commitment underlying Nina's dream gives to her ambition a positive, constructive character, whereas Almayer remains caught in egotistic, material, and racial considerations that interfere with the direct engagements and responses of his being even in relation with his daughter.

This is especially obvious at the supposed death of Dain Maroola. There is no grief in Almayer for a life that has ended prematurely and sordidly. He is distressed only because of the negative results of that death for his own business interests. His fear of going mad in consequence of his intensive mental suffering reminds the reader of King Lear, who through pain grows to the perception of other people's plights. Almayer remains concentrated on himself in self-pity and anger, and therefore ignorant of his daughter's inner conflicts. He feels shattered, but the walls around the construct of his egotistic dream remain intact. He does not become more truly human, nor does he learn to know and accept himself.

The racist and materialistic approach to life which makes Lingard assure Almayer that the dollars would cover up the color of his wife's skin is the basis on which Almayer has built his dream. Most white men in Conrad's colonial settings share the idea of a specific white-men identity. In Almayer's case it results not only in his own isolation, frustrated marriage, and miserable end, but also in his daughter's dilemma of having to choose between divided loyalties.

Nina bears the burden of her parents' mutual hatred without sharing the sentiments from which they arise; she has illusions neither about the Malays nor about the Europeans. She sees "the same manifestation of love and hate and sordid greed chasing the uncertain dollar in all its multifarious and vanishing shapes" among the ones as well as among the others (43). Nina recognizes the hypocrisy of the latter as contrasted by the "savage, uncompromising sincerity" of the former with which her own nature more readily identifies itself.

When she expresses scorn for Reshid and all Arabs, calling them cowards, it is therefore more a manifestation of her passionate being than of racial prejudice. Likewise, the fierce hatred of white people which she voices to the Dutch officers is explained by an apprehension for her lover and by her own experiences in Singapore more than by an attitudinal preference for one color of the skin over the other.

Conrad's frequent use of 'savage' in these texts has made him suspect of sharing the racist thinking of his white characters. An examination of the meanings which he attaches to the word 'savage' can exonerate him. It shows a great variety of connotations ranging from fierce, wild, untamed to unself-conscious, unspoilt, uninhibited. The fact that Almayer thinks of himself as being condemned to a "savage state of life" in Sambir is the best proof that to Conrad the word does not necessarily carry racial implications.

Nina's hunger for life and the immediacy of her response to it explain the strong influence her betel-chewing mother has on her. She is fascinated by her mother's temperamental outbursts when Almayer refuses to share his supposed knowledge about gold deposits with Lakamba. The author fittingly compares the woman's rage to volcanic eruptions, for, underlying this image is the awareness that such eruptions clear craters and lay bare passages to the heart of the earth. The picture Nina sees as her mind follows her mother's reminiscences contrasts too strongly with her father's ineffectual dream not to stimulate her imagination. To Nina, Dain Maroola is the realization of that picture.

Nina's choice of her Malay heritage as that of her identity is therefore the doing of her father as much as it is due to her mother's influence and her lover's attraction. To Almayer, Nina has never become an individual with a future of her own. She is as much a means to a goal—even if in a subtler way—as Dain Maroola. Consequently Nina's personality remains untouched by her father's plans for and with her. She does not recognize herself in them and, although her father's grief pains her, she can look on the collapse of his dream with indifference.

The author leaves no doubt that her happiness with Dain is overshadowed by the mystery she poses to the Malay because she is a white man's daughter. But her passion develops into a love that is ready to give and to forego. From this she derives courage and the determination to resist her father's appeals to pity him and to share his perverted self-respect. It also assures her that she will successfully overcome possible obstacles to her young love.

Racial prejudice in its various manifestations is not restricted to the white characters in the novel. Although Malays and Arabs unite in destroying Almayer, they have little love for each other. Both return Almayer's haughtiness with contempt for white men's physical strengths and moral weaknesses, for their follies that deafen them to the voice of reason, for their hypocrisies, rashness of temper, and lack of gratitude, but they neither respect nor trust each other. Dain speaks of Arabs as liars; Abdulla curses Babalatchi as a "wily dog," and his nephew distrusts Malays for the same reason that Dain distrusts Arabs. The Arabs condescend to visit Malays and the white man only in the darkness of night for fear of harming their reputation.

Despite his contempt for these people, Almayer does not disdain to have business dealings with them. Lingard considered wealth a safegard against racial discrimination when he assured Almayer that the dollars would cover up the color of his wife's skin. For Almayer, even the faint hope of gain suffices to make him temporarily disregard the skin of his partner.

Since from the start his dream is based on trust in wealth, gold looms large in *Almayer's Folly*. It is less concrete than the silver of the mine in *Nostromo*—for, throughout the novel it remains a fixture in the minds of those who desire it—its influence is nevertheless equally corrupting. In Conrad's fiction trust in wealth that is obtained by means other than honest work and courage is a symptom of decadence. Ironically, despite their sense of being superior on account of their white skin, Lingard and

Almayer are as much subject to the rumors about fabulous treasures in the central mountains as the Malays, or even more so. Both exploit their quality of being white, on account of which they have easier access to the interior, for the ultimate purpose of tearing out gold from the mountain, even if they do so in intention only. In this they resemble Kurtz, who tears out ivory from the virgin forest in Africa.

The juxtaposition of trust in material gain to the life of daring action serves to underline a falling-off of the characters who rely on the former and thereby to establish a point of reference for measuring Almayer's dream of wealth. Captain Lingard indulges in the passion of prospecting for gold in the interior of Borneo only after age has weakened his judgment. In a similar manner the one-eyed statesman Babalatchi ends his reflection on his and Lakamba's situation with the admission that the time of courageous action is over and prudent cunning now has to provide the means for their remaining days.

Like racial discrimination, greed is not only the white men's vice. Desire for material gain underlies the intrigues of Abdulla and Lakamba against Almayer and against each other. It leads to betrayal and to commercial rivalry. Arabs and Malays are united in fighting the native tribes in the interior for the purpose of gaining access to natural resources. But Lakamba feels no compunction when he encourages the illegal gunpowder trade between Almayer and Maroola behind Abdulla's back for the profits he hopes to reap from it. The Arab, in turn, does not hesitate to betray Lakamba's involvement in it to the Dutch authorities for a similar purpose, although earlier he was a welcome instrument in the hands of the Rajah to ruin the white man's trade and to strengthen his own position. As the novel opens, Lingard & Co. is no longer of any consequence. But Almayer continues to be Abdulla's potential rival on account of the knowledge of gold deposits which he is believed to have and in which Almayer himself believes. "Ah! my friend Abdulla . . . we shall see who will have the best of it after all these years!" (18), he exclaims in the opening chapter.

An answer to this outburst is the ironic note of regret on which Abdulla's visit to the deceased Almayer ends as the novel closes. Similar to the lieutenant who has shot the last priest in Graham Greene's *The Power and the Glory*, Abdulla finds life flat and empty when the edge is removed that rivalry has given it. His trade is flourishing; he has ingratiated himself with the Dutch authorities. But the realization at which he arrives shows him betrayed by his earlier ambitions. Confronted with his approaching end, he finds no comfort in his gains.

Greed is also at the root of the deception that prepares Nina's elopement. Repeatedly Mrs Almayer is called "witch-like." The image she creates when Nina finds her in ecstasy bent over the chest in which she hoards her dollars consolidates that reputation. Significantly, only Mrs Almayer enjoys the fruit of her greed to the end. Babalatchi and Lakamba are fined by the Dutch and, in consequence, pass their old days with reduced means and still more limited hopes; Abdulla's material fortunes have become unattractive. The picture of Mrs Almayer as an old hag who greedily guards her buried hoard, with which the novel leaves the reader, is Conrad's concluding comment on this theme.

Since to Almayer moral behavior is bound up with the faithful observance of principles based on the prejudice of white superiority and a materially conditioned social status, he considers it part of his parental duty to inculcate them also in his daughter. On the occasion of Abdulla's proposal that Nina marry his nephew Reshid, Almayer for the first time has to realize the gap between his own and Nina's standards. The wealth and the prestige Abdulla offers—which were decisive in his own choice of a mate—hold no attraction for the girl. Still, it is only after her elopement that the totality of his failure to make her follow his own principles comes home to him: "I am not of your race," his daughter tells him. "Between your people and me there is . . . a barrier that nothing can remove" (179).

In most cases, but especially in that of Almayer, racial consciousness is bound up with the question of loyalty and betrayal. Almayer's inability to employ his reason and imagination in order to free himself from the prejudices of his parental home makes him their shiftless victim. To him, any concession to Nina's love for a Malay is a breach of loyalty to his race and a betrayal of his own identity. But due to his marriage to a Malay woman and his illegal pacts with Lakamba and Dain Maroola, he has become guilty of hypocrisy and thereby undermined the claims he makes on Nina. His last and worst self-betrayal is the attempt to erase his love for his daughter from his life. With this determination he touches the roots of his being, because after the disappearance of Lingard he has made her his sole reason for existence.

According to Almayer's principles, both his daughter and her lover are guilty of betrayal. Nina's resistance to demoralizing pity does not diminish her affection for her father, however, nor the ability to distinguish between the loyalties she owes. She genuinely grieves when she causes pain to her unrelenting father in order to follow her dream. By the truthfulness to herself in doing so, she contrasts most significantly with Almayer who betrayed himself in his marriage.

The infidelity of which Almayer accuses Dain Maroola is as much the result of his own doing as it is the young man's fault. Dain pursues his own interests in trading with Almayer and in his return to Sambir after the loss of his brig. However, he has come to Almayer as a potential friend and only because his offer of friendship is rejected does his action assume the character of insincerity. Moreover, Almayer's view of Dain is inflated by the dishonesties on which his dream of wealth is based and of which he tries to make Dain a part. This is suggested by Dain's head cover, which to Almayer resembles a "fantastically exaggerated mushroom." It is a visualization of the unrealistic hopes he puts in the young Malay. Like the mushroom, these hopes lack substance and collapse the following morning.

The disastrous consequences of Almayer's inability to transcend his narrow prejudices in order to respond to the promptings of his heart serve once more to underline the theme at the end of the novel and to bring it to a conclusion. There is much irony in the fact that Almayer is fully aware of the pain he causes his daughter when he forces her to choose between himself and her lover and of the promises Nina's future holds. He could achieve his dream of distinction and greatness for Nina in a way different from his own plans: "Great things could be done! What if he should suddenly take her to his heart, forget his shame, and pain, and anger, and—follow her! What if he changed his heart . . . and made her life easier between the two loves that would guard her from any mischance!" (192). But he does not make his dream viable; instead he adheres to his perverted principles and resists the urgings of his heart. He chooses a slow and lonely death in Sambir from whose poverty and isolation he had hoped to escape. His dream becomes his folly indeed.

The consequences of Nina's choice are not unfolded within the novel, as are those of her father. But as the narrator has made sure in the opening chapter that the drifting log would reach the sea, so he confirms at the end that Nina has obtained the goal for which she has followed Dain; she has given birth to a son. In the indigenous society of this novel, this is equal to having achieved status and the immortality that is ensured through descendants.

Within the context of all three Lingard novels the news about Nina's birth of a son, a grandson to the Rajah of Bali, is weighty with larger implications. Writing to William Blackwood about his new novel, *The Rescue*, in September 1897, Conrad communicated that "in the 70[ies] Lingard had a great if occult influence with the Rajah of Bali" (CL I 383). As it has been seen earlier that the fictional Tom Lingard is closely shaped after the historical William Lingard, there is, in the author's imagination, a link also between the fictional Nina and the historical Rajah.

The tie which Nina has formed with him by choosing his son as her partner in life is a transfer and an affirmation of the one Lingard has established with the Malay leader in earlier years. It means that in her choice Nina not only counteracts the prejudices of her father but also corrects the value system of Lingard, who likewise has envisioned for her a future of wealth in Europe. Thus the turn the author has given to Nina's life by directing it to the Malay court, for the continuity of which he provides with an heir, is Conrad's expression of his belief in the values it represents.

III CHARACTERIZATION THROUGH IMAGERY

The general mood that is created in the opening chapter of *Almayer's Folly* is one of passivity, neglect, and decay. Almayer is absorbed in his unrealistic mental preoccupations, and the setting is marked by the consequences of his lacking care. Similar to her father, Nina Almayer is mentally preoccupied and not in touch with her immediate surroundings. The uprooted tree that floats down the river and arouses Almayer's envy likewise appears to be a passive victim of circumstances.

Despite these surface impressions of inertia and abandonment, there are strong undercurrents in the chapter that witness to the presence of contending forces: the conflict of Almayer's external compliance with Lingard's demand and his internal revolt against the suggested marriage, the incompatible dreams of father and daughter and the discrepancy between their dreams and the realities of their lives, the conflicting hopes and interests of Almayer and Dain Maroola and their contrasting attitudes toward racial differences.

As a reflection of the father-daughter antithesis, the form in which Conrad discusses the theme of imperialism in this novel, this introductory note of overt and covert contentions is repeated throughout it. Underneath the surface of passivity and sluggishness of life in the tropical setting, rivalling forces affect all relations and assert themselves with more or less success. Beginning with the most personal relations of husband and wife, parent and child, lover and beloved, to the most distant ones of political loyalties and trade engagements, all are characterized by actual or attitudinal self-assertions and strife.

These are visualized by the key image, the floating tree, whose weight and bulk effect the friction with the rushing waters that carry it along. Like it, much of the novel's imagery contributes to the building up of the composite effect of an all-pervading atmosphere of tensions and rivalry. In addition to this general purpose, most of the images serve a specific one. There is imagery that objectifies central ideas and values, that reflects relationships, and that in the first place reveals character and personality.

Conrad's extensive use of imagery for character presentation is due to his tendency to be descriptive rather than dramatic. The result of using this method is suggestive and often vivid, but it keeps the reader at a distance and obscures as much as it reveals; the characters remain indistinct and remote. Seen from the aspect of the author's development as a writer, this is significant since throughout his literary career, his strength remained in being descriptive.

It has been seen that the center of Almayer's dream is the idea that wealth is liberating and elevating. Hudig and Lingard, the wealthiest men he knows, are titans to young Almayer. This allusion to Greek mythology and to divine power not only denotes the place money takes in his life but also the control it exerts on him. Within the narrative of this novel—after Captain Lingard has failed him—Almayer hopes to achieve wealth first through the British Borneo Company, for which he builds his new house, and then by finding gold and diamond deposits in the interior of Borneo. Together with the floating tree, the legendary mountain of gold and the already decaying "new house" are the most pervasively effective images in the novel.

In its inaccessibility the Gunong Mas is the objective correlative of the aspirations of those who want to enrich themselves through it. The mountain's location is in the interior of Borneo, just as the idea and desire of wealth is central to the lives of most men in the novel: Lingard and Almayer, Lakamba and Babalatchi, and the natives of the coastal regions. Abdulla seems unaffected by its promises, because his wealth is already secured. But he joins Lakamba in armed expeditions against the upriver Dyak and then betrays him to the Dutch authorities, which shows that he, likewise, is motivated by expectations of still greater gain.

Mrs Almayer joins the general scramble for loot, but her interest in the Gunong Mas is relative to her relations with Lakamba; personally she is after the silver that Dain pays for the woman he loves. This association of silver with women is supported by the silver effect that the moon creates in contrast to the gold tinge of the setting sun on the river, which Almayer likes to watch. Within the context of the study of Conrad's treatment of female characters, this is of interest since unlike the elusive gold, silver is concrete and real in the novel. It is mentioned only half so often as gold, but on all those occasions when actual business is transacted—in Hudig's office, in Dain's dealing with Lakamba, and as dowry for Nina.

The young lovers are immune to the lure of the mountain. Dain has agreed to join an expedition to reach it exclusively for the purpose of obtaining gunpowder; what the mountain offers is of no interest to him. Because of the wealth which they constitute for each other, Dain and Nina remain outside its magic circle: "You were speaking of gold then," the girl tells her father, "but our ears were filled with the song of our love, and we did not hear you" (179). Only indirectly the mountain and what it stands for affect also their lives through the greediness of Lakamba and the Almayers, which provides them with opportunities for courtship and isolates them in a world of their own.

Corresponding with the symbolic meaning of the Gunong Mas are those occasions when jewelry and ornaments assert their corrupting power: Dain's rich outfit that arouses Mrs Almayer's greed, the jewelry that bribes Mahmat, and ornaments as symbols of authority that are to secure an opportunity for Babalatchi to get rid of Almayer, the inconvenient rival.

The corruption which the legendary mountain of gold causes among most of the novel's characters is emphasized by the effect of the setting. According to the description of Norman Sherry, Berau was less lawless and wild than the setting into which the author has changed it. Its function in *Almayer's Folly* can justly be called an early version of that of "Heart of Darkness." Sambir is a place that encourages lawlessness—slave trade, warfare with and among native tribes, smuggling of gunpowder, intrigue and deceit—by the impenetrability of the jungle surrounding it and the difficulty in navigating the river that connects it with the outside world.

The protagonist's moral isolation as an ineffectual dreamer who thinks himself superior to all others is emphasized by the isolated location of his house. He lives on the lower tip of the island that is formed by two branches of the Pantai river. The economic success of his rival Abdulla is visible in the elevated, spacious residence which is firmly built on a cliff on the opposite end of the island. The stronghold of Lakamba, Rajah of Sambir, finally, is across the main branch of the Pantai and opposite to Almayer's house. In this way, Conrad completes the triangle of the central contending forces.

Corresponding with these are the less covert elements that work together to undermine the lives of the inhabitants of Sambir—the settlement's distance from civilization, its unhealthy climate, the threatening jungle, and the lure of natural resources that has attracted settlers who are incompatible with each other.

In harmony with the symbolic implications of the setting, all the decisive events of *Almayer's Folly* happen under cover of darkness. Abdulla comes at night to propose marriage between Reshid and Nina; Dain Maroola arrives in Sambir at the end of the day and then visits Almayer and meets Nina for the first time; his repeated interviews with Lakamba take place at night; that is also the time when business is transacted between the Rajah and Abdulla; Dain returns to Sambir under the cover of darkness; the same night his decisive encounter with the Rajah takes place; it is followed by the fatal accident of his boatman which results in preserving his freedom and causes the collapse of Almayer's dream; Nina elopes from her parental home during the following night, and then the couple escape from Sambir. Only Babalatchi is repeatedly seen on his trips across the river and in Almayer's compound in the glaring sun of the noon hours. The one-eyed statesman is sufficiently fortified in his sly diplomacy not to need the cover of the night for his shady transactions.

River and sea are heavily charged with symbolic implications. The Pantai is generally seen as standing for life and reality (Boyle 26). It brings the lovers together and carries them toward their goal. But it also is the passage that opens up the interior to greed and exploitation. It connects and it separates. It is as murky and unreliable, at times even as deadly, as life in Sambir proves to be. Together with Almayer, the river carries Dain and Nina toward the sea, but only the young people embark on a journey across it while Almayer gazes at it from the distance. With his rejection of the lovers, he refuses to assume his share in the struggles and risks of human existence and relations for which the sea stands with its everchanging surface and its cold, cruel depths.

Much has been said about nature imagery in *Almayer's Folly*. Most critics agree that Conrad's handling of it is one of the weakest points in his early works (Boyle 26, Yelton 215). Nevertheless, its functional importance is undeniable. J.I.M. Stewart goes so far as to consider external nature "a sinister and alarming mystery" that constitutes "the central emotional focus of the novel" (39). Its function is both general and specific; it creates atmosphere and reflects a tendency towards violence and decay, but it also functions as the objectification of individual emotional states and dispositions of characters.

It certainly constitutes an important means to reveal the emotional focus of the part Nina plays in *Almayer's Folly*. Her personality is consistently revealed by a striking contrast of white and dark in her appearance. Invariably she is clad "all in white," but her dark eyes are turned toward darkness in nearly all the key scenes. They gaze into the night of the river, of the dark forest beyond the settlement, of her mother's passion—always past the person of her father to whom her words are addressed. Like her apparel, which, after her departure, her father sets on fire with the bungalow, the civilization and education to which she has been exposed is easily discarded. Her native tendency is toward the dark forces of nature with which she is in close communion when she makes solitary excursions on the river and when the tropical vegetation witnesses her passion and love for Dain.

It suggests that the principle of struggle that characterizes life in Sambir is inherent also in Nina's choice. The vitality and abundance of the thriving vegetation is coupled with deadliness; underneath the healthy growth there is victimization and disintegration. Dain returns to Sambir, despite the danger of being apprehended by the Dutch, to claim Nina, "his property." And she, in turn, feels the triumph of victory when she sees Dain at her feet: "The thing was done . . . The man was her slave" (172). Nina trusts that she holds the "bravery and strength" of the young man in her hands; at the same time she is aware that later there may be other women in Dain's life. She is prepared to measure herself with them.

Frequently nature imagery expresses relationships of varying dimensions. Storms announce or discharge themselves whenever issues of importance cause tensions among the novel's characters. Nor does the mention of Sambir's sunshine suggest happiness and harmony. Moreover, it is heavily charged with Conrad's view on imperialism as voiced in his "Note" to the novel:

> The picture of life, there as here, is drawn with the same elaboration of detail, colored with the same tints. Only in the cruel serenity of the sky, under the merciless brilliance of the sun, the dazzled eye misses the delicate detail, sees only the strong outlines, while the colors, in the steady light, seem crude and without shadow. Nevertheless it is the same picture. (vii)

On a small scale, Almayer's life in Sambir is an illustration of this passage, for throughout the novel he remains dazzled by the initial promise of his connection with Lingard and the trust he puts in his white skin. In consequence he never sees the realities of his situation clearly. When the tropical sunshine is mentioned, it is therefore mostly an ironic allusion to Almayer's inability to perceive important truths, for instance, the elements at work between mother and daughter after Nina's return from Singapore, the relation between the lovers, the intention of Babalatchi who comes to poison him, the identity of the corpse found in the river, the values he rejects with his daughter, the fact that he cannot erase the past by extinguishing its vestiges, and the inhumanity that triumphs with the rejection of love.

Mostly the moon is as unsympathetic as the sun. Its cold rays brighten up the scene when the Dutch officers enjoy themselves at the expense of Almayer; they expose the hiding place of Dain and endanger his safety, and they mercilessly ridicule the humbled, broken Almayer: "In the increasing light of the moon . . . a caricature of the sleeping Almayer appeared on the dirty whitewash of the wall behind him in a grotesquely exaggerated detail of attitude and feature enlarged to a heroic size" (157-8).

The passage is a good example of Conrad's revelation of character through setting. The sordidness of Almayer's surroundings and the distortion of his shadow to the size in which he likes to think of himself increase the irony of his self-image as a tragic victim of circumstances. An earlier scene showing him in a white jacket and flowered sarong among Dutch officers in uniforms suggests that he is as estranged from the people whose nationality he claims as he is from the natives of Sambir. But on a large scale, Almayer is characterized by his two houses. Both the old bungalow and the unfinished new building witness to his dreams; they are the settings of most of the scenes in which we meet him, and they objectify the characteristic traits of his personality—his ambitions and his feebleness of effort and purpose. Throughout the novel, we see Almayer in the light they throw on his life.

The symbolic function of Almayer's bungalow is established in the opening chapter; it finds completion in the penultimate one when after Nina's departure and his wife's desertion, Almayer sets the house on fire. The original attractiveness of the old house's construction makes visible the gain his marriage was to bring him without counting his wife in; in the same way its neglect and decay reflect the effect life in Sambir has on Almayer's morals and dreams; his initially high-flown ambitions are soon stifled and in ruins, though not dead. Nina's rocking chair is the most prominent piece of furniture, because her ability to bear the tensions of her home with seeming equanimity endows her with a superiority that awes her father. At her elopement with Dain, the chair is crushed to pieces in consequence of the effect the news has on Almayer. When he flings the key to the house into the river, he means to sever forever his ties with what the house stands for—his dream and the realities of his past.

His foolishness in attempting to forget his daughter is reflected in the setting he chooses to achieve this task. He built the "Folly" larger than the first house, because with Nina's return from Singapore his regained interest in life was inflated by the role Nina was to play in the realization of his dream. As neither father nor daughter could share the other's vision, however, the house has remained uncompleted and uninhabited. The pitfalls which it places for Almayer when he leaves it in the opening chapter show the unreliabilty of the supports on which he has based his hopes: vague notebook entries, exhausted finances, collaboration with people whom he mistrusts and despises. The house is illuminated for the first time when a court of inquiry is held in it by the Dutch officers on the night of Dain's supposed death. However, its brightness is lost on Almayer; he does not recognize the foolishness of rejecting the Malay. In consequence, more than ever before, the house is an objectification of Almayer's folly when living in it he waits for forgetfulness while all the fibres of his heart cling to the memory of his daughter. Only opium finally turns folly into the delight that allows Almayer to find forgetfulness in death.

The involvement of the Chinese Jim-Eng in bringing about Almayer's deliverance from the world of harshly conflicting realities is of interest less on account of what it reveals of Almayer than for the light it throws on the Chinese. "Patient" the narrator calls him. But there is more to Jim-Eng than endurance when he stays at Almayer's side to the end while Captain Ford turns away from him in disgust. *An Outcast of the Islands* introduces Ford as the owner of the schooner which Lingard chartered after the loss of his brig *Flash*, and in *Almayer's Folly* it is implied that Ford has succeeded to Lingard's position in the Company. But he takes no steps to remove Almayer from his sordid setting in order to change his condition. Whatever one may think of Jim-Eng's assistance to his neighbor, it is more than the white man, who remarks that an early death is the best remedy for Almayer, is ready to offer.

The father's loss is the lover's gain. Dain Maroola's first introduction in the novel as a jewelry-bedecked trader-prince is indicative of his role in the lives of most characters in *Almayer's Folly*. Like the prince of fairy tales, who comes to rescue the enchanted princess, Dain Maroola appears in the unhealthy, depressing setting of Sambir as a light-bringing savior. His European-rigged vessel, white boat, and sparkling outfit are ominous.

All with whom he comes in contact expect some gain from their relationship with Maroola. Almayer and Lakamba-Babalatchi look on him as a potential instrument to gain access to the legendary treasure in the interior of the island; Abdulla-Reshid expect to obtain favors from the Dutch by informing on Dain; Mrs Almayer schemes to enrich herself by making her daughter available to him; and the two girls, Nina and Taminah, look to Dain for love and happiness.

To make the Dain-Nina relationship more of a foil to Almayer's approach to life, the young prince—similar to the older man years earlier—finds a rival in an Arab due to the vain attempt of Abdulla to gain Nina as a bride for his nephew shortly before Maroola's arrival.   What Reshid is lacking in Nina's eyes, the Malay prince possesses in abundance. Dain is courageous and passionate; he dares to express himself "with all the unrestrained enthusiasm of a man totally untrammelled by any influence of civilized self-discipline" (64). Thus Dain carries off the prize, Nina, although Reshid succeeds in foiling the first purpose for which he has come to Sambir. In spite of his diplomatic secrecy about the nature of his trade, the Arabs outdo him in these matters. Like Almayer, Dain is defeated by them, but unlike him, Dain does not accept defeat. With his return to Sambir to fetch his bride, Dain affirms life and love as his primary value.

This obviously is the reason why the author rewards him with freedom and a son. Although he is guilty of double dealings with Almayer, Dain escapes the Dutch by a hair's breadth, because he is true to himself in what he does. The words spoken by the Malay narrator in "The Lagoon" might be coming from Dain's lips: "We are of a people who take what they want . . . There is a time when a man should forget loyalty and respect" (*Tales of Unrest* 196). In the narrow setting of Sambir the contrast between the father's ineffectual dream and the lover's determination is a drastic one. It affects Nina with a sense of strength to which her own nature eagerly responds.

The character most identical with the setting of Sambir is Babalatchi, Lakamba's one-eyed prime minister. He is physically as unattractive as the settlement, morally as unscrupulous as the murky river that washes it, in his diplomacy as impenetrable as the jungle that surrounds it. His relation to the Rajah combined with his native potential renders him a unique personality which is unmatched by any other character in the novel. The epithets attached to him—"inquisitive goat," "wily dog," "one-eyed crocodile," in addition to "statesman"—vividly illustrate the range of his qualities and involvements.

Babalatchi plays a role in all the lives that are of consequence. The diversity of his engagements is matched by that of his appearances of benevolent concern, humble servitude, and detached ignorance. Little escapes his vigilance. It is he who discovers the realities of life in Sambir and makes them known to others—the love of Nina and Dain, Taminah's infatuation with the trader-prince, the truth behind Mrs Almayer's story of the accident on the river—and always he is ingenious in taking advantage of his discoveries. Only the Gunong Mas remains an elusive idol even for Babalatchi.

The use he makes of his realization that Taminah desires Dain's attention adds an unexpected dimension to his image. It provides an opportunity to catch a glimpse of the private life of Sambir's prime minister which shows him as a lusty old man of whose amorous aspirations the narrator disapproves. For, in this matter Babalatchi's sagacity fails him since, like Lingard, he equates youth with a life span rather than with an approach to life, in consequence of which he suffers financial loss due to Taminah's early death.

The old man's desires give the author a chance to add another dimension to his discussion of imperialism, because Babalatchi's acquisition of Taminah is as much an act of victimization and subjugation as the way in which Lingard decides over the life of Almayer's wife; both take advantage of a girl's plight for the gratification of their vices. Since the attitude that underlies both actions is essentially the same, these women assume representative character.

In her fierce self-assertiveness, called 'savage' by the narrator, Mrs Almayer acts on her consciousness that independent rights are due to the people from whom she has sprung and whom Lingard has tried to exterminate. Ironically her convent education and her marriage to a white man—intended by Lingard for her emancipation—sharpen rather than diminish her instinctive appreciation of her native values, according to which courageous fight proves the man. Her ability to act, even though it is mostly in a destructive way, shows her untamed vitality, by which she contrasts most significantly with her husband and Taminah. In this context the suggestion that she entertained an adulterous relationship with Lakamba and that she had the reputation of being a witch is of interest.

This, at first sight, superficial, stereotyped way of showing incompatibility of marriage and a fierce, inscrutable temperament acquires rich suggestive power within the context of a discussion of imperialist ambitions, for, in Mrs Almayer, the granddaughter of the Sultan of Sulu, Conrad demonstrates the consequences of what she experiences as violence done to her nature by the self-glorifying Lingard and the calculating Almayer. Even though in the end he uses her to comment negatively on the philosophy of materialism that motivates most characters in the novel, his belief in the vitality and strength of the people she represents is unmistakable. There is a life force in them, Conrad suggests by the fascination the mother exerts on her daughter,

that is lost to western society. It is a loss that results in the weakness
and insincerity seen in Almayer.

When Captain Lingard transfers his love from the mother to her child,
he admits that with the woman his patriarchal colonial ideal has failed.
But in Nina he repeats the mistake of wanting to tame through western
education. In her, Mrs Almayer and Taminah meet and through her they
are linked to the protagonist. After her early years of marriage, Mrs
Almayer lives in the bungalow only during the time of Nina's presence
there; she comes back to it from the riverside hut upon her daughter's
return from Singapore, and she deserts it again at Nina's elopement with
Dain. Taminah seeks Nina's company while both accept their existence
in Sambir with resignation and apathy.

Nina's apathetic attitude toward life after her return to Sambir,
emphasized by her association with Taminah, suggests that she is as
unfree and unable to act as the slave girl, because white society has
denied her a place among itself and the population of Sambir isolates her
as the white man's daughter. Only when she identifies herself as being
one with the Malay does she become free and able to prove herself alive
through action.

If in Mrs Almayer Conrad demonstrates the forces of resistance that
are awakened by the domination of others, in Taminah he shows how
such dominance can touch the vital nerve of a people and make it wither.
It is in keeping with her social status in Sambir that Taminah acquires
an identity only through her relation to Nina, Dain, Almayer, Abdulla,
and Babalatchi. Her reactions and responses to these characters give
her individuality; without the stimuli which she derives from them,
she remains unreflective and undifferentiated. Therein she contrasts
strikingly with young Mrs Almayer who, on account of her origin, is
also a slave in the eyes of her husband, but who understands herself
as his equal. Taminah's avoidance of Mrs Almayer emphasizes their
difference.

Unlike Mrs Almayer and Nina, Taminah never achieves freedom of
mind and action, because in her this ability has been stunted from the
beginning. She cannot conceive of an existence that is not subservience;
neither can she contribute to, nor tolerate, the acquisition of freedom by
others. In consequence, jealousy turns her into a deadly rival of the pair
that seek life together. In the role she subsequently assumes she parallels
and underlines that of Almayer, who speeds up his death by taking opium
when he learns that his daughter has given birth to a son. At the victory
of life, Taminah withers away. It is no mere coincidence that her death
follows shortly after the birth of Nina's son.

In Taminah Conrad shows imperialism in its darkest colors, not only because of its life-denying consequences for others, but also because by the example of the victimization which she suffers from fellow Malays, the author makes it clear that the ambitions underlying imperialism and the destructive effects following from them are to be found not only in Europe.

IV THE HEROIC PRINCIPLE AND NARRATIVE TECHNIQUE

The structure of *Almayer's Folly* is principally decided by Conrad's approach to the central idea of this novel—imperialism and its consequences shown in the contrast between Almayer and his daughter in pursuing their dreams and by the implications of the leading image. Much of the tree's destiny has worked itself out before it drifts into the center of the reader's attention. Nor is the author concerned with its future once he has assured Almayer and the reader that it will reach the sea. In similar manner, the main characters of *Almayer's Folly* are immediately present to the reader only for the span of three days. During these, decisive stages in the working out of two human destinies are shown: Almayer's disillusionment and the ultimate collapse of his dream; parallel to these, Nina's increasing trust in a future with Dain despite opposition, threats, and the disruption of intimate ties and then her departure from Sambir followed by the news that she has given birth to an heir.

Like the main theme, supporting ones are developed with care and consistency. In the opening chapter the direction of Almayer's further development has been outlined by the brief flashback that shows his background and the conditioning of his attitudes. Almayer's self-betrayal in his loveless marriage is the first consequence of his inherited trust in wealth. Its effect on him simultaneously introduces the theme of racial prejudice and of commercial rivalry, and all these themes are developed in closest interrelation with each other.

It is mainly through the skillful handling of retrospective narrative that much of the information is provided which is necessary to appreciate the happenings of the simple past. As the novel opens, Almayer indulges in a reverie about future ease and wealth in Europe. Joining him in his retrospection, the reader comes to know that part of his history that accounts for his presence in Sambir. From his day-dreaming and the new, large house, he is recalled to the reality of his existence symbolized by the old bungalow in which he lives with his wife and daughter. There Nina, Almayer's foil, is introduced and the reader ends the chapter with the conviction that both father and daughter experience life in Sambir as an imprisonment from which they dream to escape. He also senses that their dreams differ vastly in content.

Chapters two through five are a continuous flashback acquainting the reader with the history of Mrs Almayer and Nina; with Almayer's struggle when his trade has been ruined by the rivalry of Abdulla; with Babalatchi's role as Lakamba's prime minister, financial advisor and general factotum; with the slave girl Taminah; with Abdulla's proposal of marriage for Nina and Reshid, his nephew and heir; with the arrival of the prince-trader Dain Maroola; with the revival of Almayer's dream of wealth; and with the growing passion of Dain and Nina for each other.

The remaining seven chapters cover the events of the three days that result in the ultimate crushing of Almayer's dream and in the departure of his daughter from Sambir. Interspersed in the narrative of the simple past are retrospective passages of various length which provide further background information and increase suspense.

Looked at from another angle, the structure of *Almayer's Folly* is suggestive of being an implied comment on Almayer's opinion of himself as a heroic victim of circumstances. The novel consists of twelve books that show a clear separation into two halves. Books one through six sustain a note of hopefulness and expectation on behalf of Almayer, whereas beginning with book seven the reader witnesses the series of events that consistently destroy Almayer's dream step by step. In observing the number twelve and the division into two balanced parts, Conrad followed the typical epic pattern. Furthermore, by starting "in the midst of things" and reaching back to the beginning before he worked ahead to the end, Conrad likewise followed the heroic tradition. Regardless whether he did so consciously or incidentally, the irony of the anti-heroic role Almayer plays in this novel is thereby emphasized and its impact cannot be lost on the reader.

The exposition of the opening chapter promises greatness neither of character nor of action. The story's setting, marked as it is by decay and neglect, matches the description of Almayer's personality as weak-willed and ineffectual and with the allusions to his past failures, the worst of which, without doubt, is his miscalculated marriage.

The main reason, however, that Almayer cannot arouse the reader's expectancy towards his future is his inability to exercise self-criticism.

This is evident from the conclusion he draws as he evaluates his past: "He was no fool then, and he was no fool now. Circumstances had been against him" (11). Without critical self-appraisal, growth is hardly possible and little can therefore be expected from the dreamer Almayer. If Conrad nevertheless sustains the reader's interest in the story, it is because there are other characters besides Almayer who matter in the novel; even more, it is the result of Conrad's successful handling of the retrospective method of narration, as Ian Watt has pointed out (61).

The appreciative reader who is willing to put up with the weaknesses of *Almayer's Folly*—frequent overqualification, reliance on repetition for emphasis, and an excessive use of nature imagery—in order to discover its promises finds in it numerous traces of the author's developing talent. Through the repeated use of dramatic irony in the first chapter, Conrad introduces into the narrative the element of ironic incongruity as a structural reflection of thematic issues. He does so, for instance, when Almayer reassures himself of Dain Maroola's reliability, thinking that "even Malays have some sense and understand their own interest" (14) while his preoccupation with the acquisition of wealth blinds him to the consistency with which the young Malay pursues his interest in Nina. As a result, Almayer himself has to be brought to his senses in a most painful way by the development of events.

In similar manner, Almayer's meaning is worlds apart from the way his words are to work themselves out when he says, "we shall start on the day after to-morrow ... We must not lose any time" (18). Spoken in the opening chapter in reference to the planned expedition for gold, these words become replete with ironic implications as the novel develops and when, two days later, together with the fugitive Dain Maroola, Almayer takes his daughter down the river to lose her forever. While lessening the narrative's tendency towards becoming cumbersome, this technique tightens its tissues and leaves the reader with a sense of the author's balance and control of his material.

Almayer's Folly also demonstrates Conrad's first experiment in using the device of "delayed decoding," by which his impressionism distinguishes itself. The later examples of it have a less perfect but clearly recognizable model in Almayer's response to the attempt of Taminah to awaken him to the reality of his daughter's elopement with her Malay lover (158-9). During the greater part of the process by which Almayer comes to the final decoding of Taminah's message, his state of drunken sleep causes his sensation of being under the spell of a dream. But the three stages identified by Cedric Watts—impinging sense-data which remain undeciphered, first incomplete or inaccurate decoding, then accurate decoding—(44) are clearly distinguishable in this process.

At first, the sense data of Taminah's words and of her physical presence fuse with those of sight, sound and locomotion that result from Almayer's drunkenness; they remain undeciphered. Then the sense of touch fuses with that of sound as Taminah shakes Almayer's shoulder, and the result is his conclusion that he must be the victim of a nightmare seeing an apparition—an incomplete and inaccurate decoding of the sense data. Only with the crush of broken furniture and the girl's scream after he rushes at what he takes for a phantom, is he fully aware of her identity and decodes her message correctly.

In addition, more common forms of impressionism are not lacking either. The day that ends in the final destruction of Almayer's dream first through the supposed death of Dain Maroola and then through the elopement of his daughter distinguishes itself by its brilliant and, in this context, cruel sunshine. However, a "veil of mysterious blue haze" lies over the settlement that is puzzled by the rumor of Dain's violent end. Reshid, the rejected suitor of the white man's daughter, has special reason to distrust the information that has reached him concerning his rival's death. Though externally cool and detached, his passionate desires for the half-caste woman are vividly suggested by the swarms of yellow butterflies that arise before his eyes in the heat of the sun.

How much Conrad was able to make method serve his purpose is especially illustrated in chapter five which narrates Babalatchi's discovery of the love affair between Dain and Nina and—resulting from it—of Taminah's jealousy. To create an awareness of the several complications that result from that discovery the author increases his demand on the reader's attention in this chapter through greater complexity of technique. Inserted into the retrospective account we find flashbacks of a second and third degree and repeated shifts in the narrative point of view. From Babalatchi's afternoon visit to Almayer's compound, the reader is taken to the early morning of the same day when the one-eyed statesman becomes a witness to the young people's love and to Taminah's distress which results from it. From there, the reader returns to the afternoon to observe Almayer immersed in preparations for the impending expedition to find gold. This gives the narrator an opening to reach back over the last two weeks during which Almayer scarcely has taken notice of Dain, who in consequence has been free to court Nina in the mango grove. Finally he goes back to the moment of the lover's first meeting and from there he unfolds the development of their love affair in chronological order to Dain's departure and the expectancy with which father and daughter await his return at the end of the opening chapter.

Most of these time shifts are accompanied by changes in the narrative point of view. Starting out with an objective narrative as Babalatchi crosses the river, Conrad soon makes the reader aware of the sly statesman's view on his discovery of the young people's love that morning. Then he turns to the preoccupied Almayer to show the conditions of the quest for gold from the white man's point of view. For the rest of the chapter the reader listens to the omniscient narrator catching occasional glimpses of the state of affairs through Nina's eyes.

In addition to the skillful handling of time and narrative point of view, the author succeeds in keeping close control over the action by which the main theme works itself out. The crushing of the dream that occupies Almayer's mind on the evening of the opening chapter begins early the following day with the news of Dain's death. Simultaneously we are told of the daughter's yielding to the "new principle of her life" (103), which prepares her elopement with Dain. The events that lead up to it are developed parallel to Almayer's increasing degradation and the despair that grips his heart when Nina confronts him with the question, "You ask why I want to go, and I ask you why I should stay" (179). With the parting of father and daughter, development ends for Almayer. The time left to him is one of static waiting for forgetfulness and death visualized by the immobility of his countenance.

Resembling the tree that drifts into the new waters of the ocean, there is a beginning for Nina as the novel ends. Within the frame of this fiction Nina has realized her dream; her future remains untold. In the father-daughter antithesis of *Almayer's Folly*, it is significant that the news of her success—of a child having been born—hastens Almayer's death through his resorting to opium in order to achieve forgetfulness. But the question as to the price she pays for sustaining the life she has chosen and the duration of her happiness remains unanswered. In this way the novel's ending effectively reflects the complexity of life in general and the possibilities inherent in the theme of imperialism in particular. It looks forward to those pieces of Conrad's best fiction that refuse to offer final answers to the quest of life.

AN OUTCAST OF THE ISLANDS

I THE BURDEN OF CONSCIOUSNESS

With the completion of *Almayer's Folly* early in 1894, a period of depression, ill health, and anxiety began for the author. As his further career shows, it was a mental and physical state that was to develop into a pattern at the completion of each new work. His manuscript of *Almayer's Folly* was with T. Fisher Unwin in London, to whom he had sent it on July 4 and from whom he anxiously expected a reply. At the beginning of August, he left London for Champel-les-Baines, the spa on the outskirts of Geneva whose beneficial effect he had experienced on an earlier occasion. There he hoped to find relief from his physical ailment and probably also from his worries about the reception his novel would get from the publisher.

A letter written in Champel on August 18, 1894, addressed to Mme Poradowska, announces the first beginnings of his new novel, *An Outcast of the Islands*. Conrad writes:

> I have begun to write—only the day before yesterday. I want to make this thing very short—let us say twenty to twenty-five pages, like those in the *Revue*. I am calling it 'Two Vagabonds', and I want to describe in broad strokes, without shading or details, two human outcasts such as one finds in the lost corners of the world. A white man and a Malay. You see how the Malays cling to me! I am devoted to Borneo. What bothers me most is that my characters are so true. I know them so well that they shackle the imagination. The white is a friend of Almayer—the Malay is our old friend Babalatchi before he arrived at the dignity of prime minister and confidential adviser to the Rajah. There they are. But I can't find a dramatic climax.

. . . Do you think one can make something interesting without
any women?! (CL I 171)

This passage is of interest for a number of reasons. Like the first
version of *Almayer's Folly* and the original plan for *Lord Jim* (Najder
258), the author's original conception of this story did not provide for
significant female characters. The passage also shows how the story
of Willems grew far beyond his creator's first plan, which may be
worth considering when the causes of what occasionally is referred to as
Conrad's loss of control in writing *Lord Jim* are discussed. Furthermore,
the passage is an example of the gaps between Conrad's presen⁺ tion of
events—or the reader's understanding of what he says about himself—
and the things that actually happened. In his "Author's Note" to *An
Outcast*, Conrad creates the impression that the novel was written in
response to Edward Garnett's encouraging remark, "You have the style,
you have the temperament; why not write another?" "I remember,"
Conrad writes, "that on getting home I sat down and wrote about half
a page of '*An Outcast of the Islands*' before I slept" (viii). He may
well have done so, but what he wrote was not the beginning of his
new novel. According to Garnett, their first meeting occurred only in
November after, in a letter of September 8, he had communicated to Mme
Poradowska that he had "burned much" of the "two vagabonds" (CL I
174). This suggests that before his return to London, this new piece of
fiction had already occupied a considerable amount of Conrad's attention
and time.

It is nevertheless true that E. Garnett contributed essentially to the
making of Conrad's second novel. In the introduction to his edition
of letters written to him by the author, Garnett recalls how from the
beginning "Conrad's attitude to *An Outcast* was . . . a strange blend
of creative ardor and skepticism" (7). The statement is supported by
the evidence in Conrad's letters in which references to his work on *An
Outcast* are crowded with expressions of doubts and dark moods that
wanted to be relieved by encouragement. Garnett was ready to offer it
and thereby urged the author to forge ahead. "For many, many hours I
sat with Conrad in those early years," Garnett writes, "trying to assuage
his doubts, fears and anxieties about his writing powers" (20).

The scepticism of the developing author did not allow him to devote
himself to his literary occupation with an undivided attention. The sea
still kept calling him and he hoped to return to it by securing the command
of a ship. Although on October 10 he expressed the intention to sell
the manuscript of the new novel to T. Fisher Unwin (CL I 180), on

October 23 he confessed that he lacked concentration on the story. "I am discouraged," he wrote. "Ideas don't come. . . . To be honest, I am busy with my plans for leaving, and, as they seem unlikely to mature, I am in a state of irritation which does not allow me to lose myself in my story—consequently, the work is worthless" (CL I 182).

Nevertheless, the novel grew and by the end of the month he had finished the first three chapters. This is evident from the fact that in a letter dated October 29 or November 11, he expresses his inablity to work saying, "the page has stayed blank except for a 'IV' at the top. I am really on the wrong path" (CL I 185). The same letter shows that meantime he had arrived at a more detailed and changed conception of the plot, in which the importance of Babalatchi's role was modified and Aïssa introduced. After venting his anger about Mrs M. Wood, whom he accused of having stolen his title because her recently published book was called *The Vagabonds*, he outlines the main idea of the novel as follows:

> the theme is the unrestrained, fierce vanity of an ignorant man who has had some success but neither principles nor any other line of conduct than the satisfaction of his vanity. In addition, he is not even faithful to himself. Whence a fall, a sudden descent to physical enslavement by an absolutely untamed woman. I have seen that! The catastrophe will be brought about by the intrigues of a little Malay state where poisoning has the last word. The dénouement is: suicide, again because of vanity.

He adds that in order to meet the requirements of Unwin's Pseudonym Library he would limit its length to 36,000 words (CL I 185). The finished novel exceeds the originally planned length by about three times, and it does not contain the suicide that Conrad had intimated in his letter. But in most other respects the main story follows this outline.

In the following weeks Conrad was troubled by poor health and in a letter of early December he wrote: "For the previous fortnight I have not written a single word. It's all over, it seems to me. I feel inclined to burn what there is. It is very poor! Too Poor! This is my profound conviction and not a cry of stupid modesty. I have struggled like that for a long time" (CL I 189). But in the middle of the month, he reassured Mme Poradowska saying, "I have burned nothing. One talks like that, but then one lacks the courage. . . . there is always something lacking, sometimes strength, sometimes perseverance, sometimes courage. . . . I am working a little. I agonize with pen in hand. Six lines in six days" (CL I 191).

By the end of the year, the author's developing friendship with E. Garnett began to bear fruits. Conrad occupied himself more fully with the writing of his second novel. He had chosen its present title to replace the original one, and he had completed eight chapters, expecting to finish the work by adding four more (CL I 193). "*The Outcast, etc. etc.* goes on its foolish little way in the midst of the usual wailing and gnashing of teeth," he wrote to Poradowska in February 1895 (CL I 202). In the middle of March he expressed much satisfaction to Edward Garnett for the way this friend had read his manuscript: "To be read—as you do me the honour to read me—is an ideal experience—and the experience of an ideal; . . . Your appreciation has for me all the subtle and penetrating delight of unexpected good fortune" (CL I 205). On May 1, Conrad wrote to the same recipient, "I am going to look for Willems in Switzerland. . . . Seriously, I find I can't work. Simply can't! I am going to try what mountain air combined with active fire-hose (twice a day) will do for divine inspiration . . . maybe the lenient gods will allow me to finish that infernal Manuscript" (CL I 211-12).

Gratifying reviews of *Almayer's Folly*, which Conrad meantime was receiving, had a favorable effect on him and eventually helped towards the completion of the new novel. "I have set my affairs in order," he wrote to Poradowska on June 11, "and I have gone back to writing, strongly encouraged by *seven and a half* columns in the *Weekly Sun*, where T.P. O'Connor has buried me under an avalanche of compliments, admiration, analysis, and quotations" (CL I 229).

During August, a variety of engagements made a claim on Conrad's time, as is obvious from his letter to E.L. Sanderson written on August 24 (CL I 238-42) and, on September 17, he finally could announce that *An Oucast* was finished. "It is my painful duty," he wrote to Garnett,

> to inform you of the sad death of Mr Peter Willems late of Rotterdam and Macassar who has been murdered on the 16th inst at 4 p.m. while the sun shone joyously and the barrel organ sang on the pavement the abominable Intermezzo of the ghastly Cavalleria. As soon as I recovered from the shock I busied myself in arranging the affairs of the two inconsolable widows of our late lamented friend and I am glad to say that—with the help of Captain Lingard who took upon himself all the funeral arrangements—everything was decently settled before midnight. You know what strong affection I had for the poor departed so you won't be surprised to hear that to me—since yesterday life

seems a blank—a dumb solitude from which everything—even the shadows—have completely vanished.

Almayer was the last to go, but, before I succeeded in getting rid of him, he made me perfectly wretched with his grumblings about the trouble and expense connected with the sad event and by his unfeeling remarks about the deceased's little failings. He reviled also Mrs Willems, who was paralysed with grief and behaved more like a cumbersome dummy than a living woman. I am sorry to say he wasn't as sober as he ought to have been in these sad conjectures and as usual he seemed not aware of anybody's grief and sufferings but his own—which struck me as being mostly imaginary. I was glad to see him go, but—such is the inconsequence of the human heart—no sooner he went than I began to regret bitterly his absence. I had for a moment the idea to rush out and call him back but before I could shake off the languor of my sorrow he was gone beyond recall. (CL I 245)

It seems that similar to *Almayer's Folly*, Conrad planned to structure this novel on the heroic principle of twelve. Although he spoke of the possibility of there being twenty or twenty-one chapters when it was clear to him that he could not confine himself to twelve (CL I 209), his first version of *An Outcast* ended with twenty-four. This is evident from Conrad's correspondence with Emilie Briquel—whose brother Paul had suggested an epigraph for *An Outcast* chosen from Victor Hugo— and with Edward Garnett. To the former he wrote on July 14, 1895: "I am now wrestling—at the closest of quarters—with chapter XXIII of my new book. Then comes Chapter XXIV and then—the deluge" (CL I 237). Edward Garnett read the concluding chapters as soon as they were finished and promptly communicated his opinion about the ending to the writer. To this Conrad responded on September 24, 1895, with the following:

You gild the pill richly—but the fact remains that the last chapter is simply abominable. . . . I am glad you like the XXIII chapter. I tell You the honest truth I like it myself. As to the XXIV I feel convinced that the right course would be to destroy it, . . . The only question is: can I? . . . Nothing now can unmake my mistake. I shall try—but I shall try without faith, because all my work is produced unconsciously . . . It isn't in me to improve what has got itself written. . . . In the treatement [sic] of the last scenes I wanted to convey the kind of placidity that

is caused by extreme surprise. You must not forget that they
all are immensely amazed. That's why they are so quiet—(At
least I wanted them to be quiet and only managed to make
them colourless). That's why I put in the quiet morning—the
immobility of surrounding matter emphasised only by the flutter
of small birds. Then the sense of their position penetrated [sic]
the[ir] hearts—stirs them.—They wake up to the reality. Then
comes violence: Joanna's slap in Aïssa's face, Willem's rush,
Aïssa's shot—and the end just as he sees the joy of the sunshine
and of life. (CL I 246-8)

As a result of Garnett's criticism, Conrad revised and rearranged,
getting the novel ready for the printers by adding two numbers to the
chapters of the book.

Conrad's agreement with T. Fisher Unwin was that *An Outcast* should
be published in November of the same year. But an unforeseen delay was
necessitated by the conflagration to which the stereo-plates of the novel
fell victim at the American printer's. In order to safeguard the copyright,
Unwin's publication had to be postponed to March 1896. By that time,
the American edition at Appleton's was expected to be ready. Although
it was not brought out until August (CL I 258n1), Unwin's edition was
published, with a dedication to E.S. Sanderson, in three thousand copies
on March 4 (Ehrsam 293).

More than in the case of *Almayer's Folly*, the reviews of the novel
ranged from loud praise to severe criticism. "Mr. Conrad's second book,
An Outcast of the Islands, bears out the extraordinary promise given by
his first romance, *Almayer's Folly*," the *Daily News* declared (CH 68);
"The remarkable promise displayed by Mr. Conrad in *Almayer's Folly* is
fully maintained in *An Outcast of the Islands*, which is unquestionably one
of the strongest and most original novels of the year," was the opinion of
the reviewer in *Athenaeum* (CH 79); the novel was said to be "brilliant,"
"remarkable," "well-told," of "indefinable power."

These voices were balanced by those that with equal strength
pointed out its shortcomings. They found it lacking in proportion and
concentration, showing tendencies towards turgidity and affectation of
style and suffering from wordiness. Conrad felt especially "chastened"
by criticism published in the *National Observer*. This he admitted in a
letter to T. Fisher Unwin on April 22, 1896, written on Ile-Grande to
where he had retired with Jessie, his newly-wed wife (CL I 276). The
National Observer wrote:

We are sorry not to be able to write more appreciatively of what
is evidently a careful and conscientious piece of work, but as it
stands, *An Outcast of the Islands* is undeniably dull. It is like one
of Mr. Stevenson's South Sea stories, grown miraculously long
and miraculously tedious. There is no crispness about it and the
action is not quick enough, a serious charge to make against a
book of adventure. Even schoolboys will probably have some
difficulty in getting through it and we fear adults will find it
impossible. (CH 70)

In his unsigned essay in *Saturday Review*, H.G. Wells analyzed
the novel's defects in great detail. He called it a "remarkably fine
romance" with a "glaring fault": "His sentences are not unities, they
are multitudinous tandems, and he has still to learn the great half of his
art, the art of leaving things unwritten." But he continued by speaking
of *An Outcast of the Islands* as perhaps "the finest piece of fiction" that
had been published in 1895, and he ended his review by stating, "Only
greatness could make books of which the detailed workmanship was so
copiously bad, so well worth reading, so convincing, and so stimulating"
(CH 73-6).

H.G. Wells' perceptive reading elicited sentiments of gratitude from
Conrad and, although still unaware of the identity of his reviewer, he
expressed them in the following words:

> I wish to thank You for the guidance of Your reproof and for the
> encouragement of your commendation. You have repeated aloud
> and distinctly the muttered warnings of my own conscience. I
> am proud to think that, writing in the twilight of my ignorance,
> I have yet seen dimly the very shortcomings which You point
> out with a hand so fine and yet so friendly. (CL I 278-9)

In writing to T. Fisher Unwin, he referred to Wells' review saying, "I
don't believe either in greatness or in the dishonour of his last paragraph.
But I am thankful to him for *all* he says. I can see the beam in mine own
eye and am not afraid to own it" (CL I 279). To Garnett, he admitted
that the review has "puzzled" him, "but," he continued, "I felt confusedly
what you say in your letter. Something brings the impression off—makes
its effect. What? It can be nothing but the expression—the arrangement
of words, the style—Ergo: the style is not dishonourable" (CL I 281).

Underlying Conrad's sincere appreciation of Wells' perceptive reading
of the novel was the fact that in contrast to most others, this review did
not speak of *An Outcast* as an adventure story for schoolboys. Conrad

resented being compared with Stevenson and Kipling; and justly so. Some attention to the themes of the novel soon makes it clear that, like in *Almayer's Folly,* the distant, exotic setting is only a background to the study of altogether different issues. The things that matter have little to do with adventure beyond the fact that the white man's presence in eastern settings required some initial readiness for adventure.

II THE WEB OF RIVALRY—
THE IMPERIAL THEME AS A COVERT PLOT

The story of Lingard's protégé in *An Outcast of the Islands* is again one of a white trader in the Malay setting. In the opening chapter, Peter Willems is introduced as a young man who lacks moral fibre. He is devoid of any sense of spiritual or social values beyond those that gratify his vanity, and with great consistency he refuses to assume responsibility for his conduct. Like Mr. Kurtz, he is hollow at the core, and since emptiness offers itself to be filled in some way, Willems' inner void provides an opening for the discussion of issues that in the colonial setting are again charged with political implications.

The undercurrents that are at work in the novel and that disclose themselves as Willems' story develops flow over into the previous novel. In this manner, *An Outcast* adds to the understanding of *Almayer's Folly*, and in consequence both are recognized as more serious discussions of imperialism than the stories of the protagonists, taken separately, would suggest. Far from being simplistic, *An Outcast* shows up the complexity of the problems that follow from European interference in the society of Sambir at the local and international level; it stimulates reflection and prepares for Conrad's most successful treatment of these themes in "Heart of Darkness."

The conclusion at which Captain Lingard arrives late in *An Outcast* is that it was a "failure of his judgment" to have established a tie with Willems (223). Earlier, Willems reflects on the cause that has cost him his privileged position in Macassar and calls it a "little want of judgment" (80); again he refers to it as an "error of judgment" after he has betrayed Lingard (266). His double repetition of the phrase, which then is echoed by Lingard, gives the scene the flavor of a musical duet and ensures

the reader's realization of its importance. The astonishment that takes
hold of Lingard at Willems' words and results in his repeating them is
only indirectly related to the events to which the speaker refers. Seeing
Willems stand before him barefoot again—as at seventeen—Lingard is
shocked into the awareness that the wheel has come full circle and that
there is a common denominator for Willems' conduct and his own; both
have called it "judgment."

It is by reliance on his judgment, however, that Lingard sentences
Willems in order to help justice assert itself.   This problematic
relationship of justice and judgment shows up the relativity of the former
and the doubt, confusion, and sense of guilt that overcome Lingard as
he warns Willems that "There is, under heaven, such a thing as justice"
(265) are its ironic results. Lingard's patronizing care and Abdulla's
greedy ambitions, like the story of Willems' hollowness, have to be seen
against this ironic incongruity between the limitations of human judgment
and what is called justice in the novel.

Significantly, the effort Lingard makes in order to penetrate to the
mystery of Willems' act of betrayal is accompanied by his recollection
of the "sweetness and strife of Carimata days" (223). Thereby Lingard integrates Willems into the larger frame of his own career as a
paternalistic colonial authority who derives his greatest satisfaction from
shaping the destinies of other people, and it becomes obvious that Willems
cannot be done full justice outside that frame, because Lingard stands at
the crossroads of Willems' life.

In this way the fact emerges that there is a dimension to this novel that
the author did not touch upon when, early in its composition, he outlined
the story in a letter to Mme Poradowska (CL I 185). It is likely that
Conrad himself was not yet aware of this wider perspective which would
explain the discrepancy between the originally planned and the actually
achieved length of the novel. Lingard clearly is of greater importance
than Conrad's outline suggests. The mere fact that the frequency of his
name in the text exeeds that of Willems by forty-five times witnesses to
the weightiness of his role in the novel. Indirectly the author also admits
the comparatively light weight of the main action at the completion of *An
Outcast* when in writing to Garnett he speaks of Willems' "little failings"
(CL I 245).

When he introduces Lingard in chapter two, Conrad implies that the
Rajah Laut had come to the East well before the general scramble of
European countries for inexpensive raw materials from the eastern seas
began. In a way, Lingard becomes a victim of the developments, for his
"straightforward simplicity of motive and honesty of aim" (13) are not

compatible with the tactics of capitalistic society that manifest themselves in the rapid expansion of steam navigation and the simultaneously developing trade competitions.

As long as his patriarchal position in Sambir remains unchallanged, however, Lingard acts on assumptions that have much in common with those of the generation that replaces him. As the novel opens, he is sufficiently established, both economically and socially, to trade for enjoyment as much as for profit. According to Sir James Brooke, it was in the interest of the local population that European traders resided in the remote areas of Borneo to collect the produce of the country in exchange for European goods (Keppel 28). This is what Lingard does in Sambir. Even though his first purpose in entering the Pantai river was his own gain, his interest in the welfare of the Malays is genuine. But the satisfaction he derives from meddling with their lives is strongly rooted in a race consciousness that considers different color of skin a visible proof of more or less highly developed human qualities, and the complications that follow from this in *An Outcast* draw wider circles than in the previous novel.

Although in *An Outcast* "Lingard's virtues are large," as P. Wiley has put it (42), and his concern for Sambir's development is sincere so that it has been taken as a proof of Conrad's belief in a viable form of colonialism (Zimmermann 37-56), Lingard is not sufficiently disinterested not to cause harm. His pride in having created peace and prosperity in Sambir, of being the absolute master there, his determination to preserve the secret of navigating the Pantai river as the key to his Arcadia, as well as his pleasure in discovering new markets for his cargoes appear to be innocent enough. But Lingard's determination to make the people of Sambir happy "whether or no" (200) and the mention of his heavy hand with which the narrator ends the account of Lingard's beginnings in Sambir are warning signals.

Looked at from the angle of European expansionism, Lingard's ambitions betray the same desire for power, influence, and gain that on a large scale has resulted in the contention of European nations for overseas territories. Almayer's observation that "there isn't a man in Sambir, big or little, who is not in debt to Lingard & Co." and the fact that Lingard is prepared to back his colonial policy by loaded rifles (171) hardly suggest that the people of Sambir enjoy Arcadian happiness. This discrepancy between the reality of the things in the settlement and the way Lingard sees them is possible, because to him O. Mannoni's finding that the colonial lacks "awareness of the world of Others" (108) is fully applicable. Furthermore, since Lingard is not given to introspection and therefore ignorant of motivations, he can only be puzzled when the natives want to get rid of him and ironically use his protégé, Willems, to achieve their goal.

The Arab who replaces Lingard is likewise a potential threat to Sambir's free development, as Babalatchi correctly surmises and soon finds confirmed. The introduction of the Arab Abdulla bin Selim equals that of the Englishman Lingard in care and length. Both are wealthy and fortunate and in consequence respected and influential. But beginning with their physical appearances—the one large and crude, of fierce aspect and boisterous in expression, the other slight and delicate, humble and dignified in bearing—they clearly are representatives of two different worlds. Lingard, whose humble origin was in Devonshire and whose first acquaintance with seafaring life was that of a boy on a Brixham trawler, is a self-made man (196). Courage, enthusiasm, and seamanlike instinct are the secrets of his success. Abdulla's fortune is inherited and its increase the fruit of a clan enterprise as much as his own doing. In this connection the observation that Aïssa acknowledges Abdulla as her kinsman is of significance (131). Finally, by putting the western limits of Abdulla's travels at the Gulf of Suez, the narrator stresses the Arab's identity as that of an Asian (109), even though Lingard speaks of him as a British subject (179). The observation of Almayer towards the end of the novel that Abdulla has settled down in Sambir for the reason that it has no white population corroborates this representative aspect of Abdulla's role.

Twice in this novel Conrad uses the modifier 'unswerving' to denote the most characteristic qualities of these two contrasting individuals. Beginning with his first journey to the Holy Shrine at seventeen (109), Abdulla's life and personality are shaped by his Islamic faith which he observes with an "unswerving piety of his heart" (109). His charity, humble bearing, and ascetic habits are strictly in keeping with his religion and limited by it. Lingard vaguely remembers the Sunday school teaching of his childhood, but his generosity and benevolence are rooted in what the narrator calls Lingard's "absurd faith in himself" (13), which allows the Rajah Laut to dispense with the mechanisms of self-protective devices and results in his "unswerving honesty" (13-4) and largeness of heart.

Between these two poles lies the field of Willems' action in Sambir, as the conclusion of the fourth chapter of part one makes clear. The mania to vie with Lingard for supremacy in the Archipelago, of which the narrator says that it is the Arab's "paramount interest in life, the salt of his existence" (111) and Lingard's pledge to keep the rival out of his river at any cost (45) relegate Willems' story to the secondary place of being a means to a goal. Despite his original conception of Willems as the bearer of the main action, Conrad has made him serve a plot of much vaster dimensions, by which Willems' role and destiny are modified.

This insight leads to the recognition of the intertextuality of the Lingard novels, which in turn results in an awareness of their being charged with the political issues of rivalry between the colonial powers of England and Holland on the one hand and material, tribal, and religious interests among the local population on the other. As a covert plot in which Captain Lingard and Abdulla figure as the main characters, the treatment of these issues connects *An Outcast* and *Almayer's Folly* with each other, and in *The Rescue* they become the subject matter of the main action.

The presence of younger protagonists in the first two novels, furthermore, results in an evaluation of the paternalistic type of colonizer of whom O. Mannoni holds that he made colonialization possible by virtue of "courage, rough justice, and simple good-humour." Compared with the figure of authority, Lingard, Almayer and Willems are seen dwarfed. But the author also examines the nature and consequences of the authority that Lingard exerts over both, his white protégés and the native population, and thereby Conrad explodes the myth of a possible Arcadia created by the white man among indigenous people.

At the heart of imperialist ambitions is the acquisition of power by way of material gain. In Conrad's terms, "imperialism" is expressed as "material interests," and when examined closely, Abdulla's ambitions are political as well as economic ones. Earlier, this has become obvious in the case of Dain Maroola. In consequence, the Arab trader is revealed as an eastern counterpart to the European imperialists, and—like passages in the previous novel—he witnesses to Conrad's view that human nature and ambitions are essentially the same in East and West.

Seen from the wide angle of intertextuality, Willems' story is only a partial answer to the question of victory and defeat in the rivalry between Abdulla and Lingard. A full one offers itself by a reading across the limits of *An Outcast* to the conclusion of *Almayer's Folly*, for Abdulla's role in the life of Almayer is an extension and continuation of his strife against Lingard, whose representative and successor Almayer is. Even though the latter is economically and morally defeated at the opening of *Almayer's Folly*, as the supposed bearer of Lingard's knowledge about gold deposits, he remains a rival in the Arab's eyes to the very end. Familiarity with both novels offers the key to Abdulla's sensation that life has turned stale when with the return of Lingard to Europe and the death of Almayer these white men have passed out of his life, because it is in *An Outcast* that the narrator offers the clue to it with the observation that, to the Arab, the challenge of an enemy is a prerequisite for an interesting and happy form of existence (111).

Even though Abdulla's sentiment is explained by the tenets of his religion which render the value of his victory at best questionable, his speedy dismissal of Willems as an instrument and ally against Lingard may seem surprising unless it is seen within the context of the larger plot, the confrontation of East and West. Separated from the latter on account of his alienation from Lingard, Willems is no longer of any interest to the Arab.

What appear to be a Moslem's scruples about dealings with an infidel is an opening for the author to confront Lingard with truths about himself and his colonial policy. As he accepts his rival's decision that Willems should be judged by his benefactor, Lingard is faced with the necessity to form a judgment on his own involvement in Willems' life.

This point in the novel's development opens up an additional aspect of Conrad's treatment of imperialism inasmuch as it shows forces at work of which neither Lingard nor Willems are aware. The fact is that both are caught in the tight meshes of the net that Abdulla's clan has spread over the Archipelago and with which Lingard has tampered when he vanquished Omar, the kinsman of the former. It is in consequence of Aïssa's experience of the strength of white men in that fight that she is fascinated by Willems' passion for her and determined to preserve her power over him. In his protégé, the bearer of his confidences, Lingard himself is caught. Thus it is not merely by chance that Omar's death coincides with the recognition of the full scope of his defeat at which Lingard arrives. This Babalatchi suggests with the question whether white men hear the voices of the dead. In spite of himself, Omar and his interests are avenged in his daughter, and as in the previous novel, the underlying idea asserts itself that, given enough time, the temporarily stifled but unbroken spirit of the indigenous people will eventually defeat the foreign powers that impose themselves. Ironically, Lingard cooperates with this development when he tells Aïssa that she shall have Willems' life (255).

He does so, because he refuses to see the issue as one of the colonized confronting the colonizer. Racial prejudice incapacitates him to look at his opponents in terms other than British and Dutch subjects and obliges him to act as the judge of Willems' conduct. Implicitly he admits to himself that in condoning Willems' weaknesses as 'sympathetic' qualities, he has contributed to what the younger man has become. The question of Willems' motivation in betraying him is a vital issue to Lingard, because he dimly recognizes a connection between that act and his own taintedness. When he nevertheless proceeds to impose a punishment, he is impelled to do so by a complexity of motivations that he does not understand. While Lingard thinks of dealing fairly by his one-time protégé and of meting out nothing but justice, he speaks of Willems as his shame. Thereby he admits that in hiding away the man who has been the cause of his pride for many years, he disowns his mistake. He does not only fail to grow through the recognition of his mistake; he lowers himself to the level of Willems who consistently disowns his misdeeds, and what Lingard calls an act of justice discloses itself as a primitive act of self-deceit.

Lingard's behavior is prompted by the need to redeem his seriously shaken faith in himself. In rejecting Willems he rejects that within himself which has led to his involvement with the young man—his unreasoning benevolence. Therefore Willems' renewed appeal to his benefactor is of no avail, and with the external rejection Lingard detaches himself from the idea of any further responsibility for that man's existence, that is, for the consequences of his own mistake.

Thus a dark shadow of doubt falls not only on Lingard's role in the life of Willems, but on all the fruits of his generous meddling with other lives, most of all on his involvement in Sambir. It is Conrad's answer to the question whether he believed in a viable form of colonialism. For, in the same way in which Lingard's taintedness interferes with consistency in backing up Willems when he needs it most, so it also refuses further concern for the inhabitants of Sambir who become the victims of the newly developing power struggle between Abdulla and Lakamba, the self-appointed new Rajah.

Moreover, with the rejection of Willems by both poles—by Abdulla, whose material gain he has enhanced, and by Lingard, whose vanity he has gratified for years—the highly politically charged question asserts itself: how much allowance should be made for the mistake of the white man. Conrad's opinion can be deduced from the doubly ironic solution to which Lingard resorts as he attempts to hide his mistake where its incongruity has become most obvious, and when with the words "you shall have his [Willems'] life," he sets up the most pronounced critic of his mistake as the judge over it (255). Thus the bullet from Aïssa's hand effects much more than the death of one white man, and the title of the novel assumes a connotation that is more inclusive than Willems' story would suggest.

Compared with those of the covert plot, the weight and scope of Willems' story are light and narrow. Although in his hollowness Willems is related to Kurtz, as Garnett suggested when he pointed out the

connection between Conrad's experience in the Congo and the creation of
the protagonist of *An Outcast* (8), Willems is not Kurtz. The unfavorable
conditions of his background, his initial insignificance, and the general
moral decay among the society of Macassar and Sambir do not allow for
the contrasts that result in the appalling effect of Kurtz's disintegration
in "Heart of Darkness." Furthermore, as Willems correctly argues,
even without his involvement it might only be a question of time for
Abdulla and Babalatchi to outwit their white rivals. But Conrad wants
his protagonist to be taken seriously, and although he leaves no doubt
that Willems is the product of contemporary European developments that
have made economic advancement the supreme value, he holds Willems
responsible for what he is.

This is implied by the fact that Abdulla and Willems are of the same
age—seventeen—when they enter society. As Conrad himself was of that
age when he left his native country, coincidence can safely be ruled out.
A consideration of the biographical data of Sir Hugh Clifford, longtime
governor of British territories in the Malay Archipelago, which Conrad
knew well (PR iii-iv), likewise speaks in favor of a conscious choice of
the age of seventeen for Willems. In a letter to the distinguished editor
and critic Edmund Gosse, Sir Clifford says of himself that for three years
he lived among Malays as nearly the only white man beginning from the
time when he was seventeen (Sept. 5, 1927, Bloomington).

It follows that Willems is meant to be seen as capable of making
decisions of his own when Lingard runs across him in Macassar and
takes him up. Though slight in appearance—a cause that stimulates the
paternalistic inclinations of the older man—with the decision to stay in
the East and later with his transfer from Lingard to Hudig, the teenage boy
and young man very directly determines some of the direction his future
takes. But it is by the association of Willems with Lingard that their
affinities become obvious—material interests as motivation for being in
the East, love of flattery, gratification derived from playing providence
for others, the sense of white superiority—and that simultaneously
Willems' falling off in stature as a colonial personality is exposed. In light
of Willems' further development in the East, the reality of their affinities
is as disconcerting as the actual achievements of his benefactor put beside
Willems' empty claim to deference and admiration are impressive.

The young man's first appeal to the "English captain" is of significance,
for at the very start it introduces the element of politics into their
relationship. Because of this the turn of the Dutchman to Hudig, likewise
a Dutch national, and later his betrayal of Lingard assume the character of

semi-public declarations against the political rival which with the hoisting of the Dutch flag in Sambir become official ones.

It is obviously no mere coincidence that early in their career both of Conrad's protagonists, Kaspar Almayer and Peter Willems, are in the service of the banker and trader Hudig, Almayer before he attaches himself to Lingard, and Willems after he has been associated with Lingard for a good period of time. In both cases there is an expectation of financial gain in the transfer from one employer to another, and for both men economic betterment is bound up with marriage to a more or less undesired woman, one the adopted, the other the natural daughter of the employer.

The degree to which Hudig's cashier, Mr. Vinck, contributes to these early developments in the lives of the protagonists, though unobtrusive, is far from negligible. Vinck is anxiously concerned about his position in Hudig's firm and the opportunities it offers him, and he is determined to bring about the removal from it of both Almayer and Willems.

Again intertextuality brings to light a covert plot, this time showing the intrigues of one white man against another. In the case of Al-mayer, psychological insight and persuasive power suffice to whet the protagonist's appetite for material gain and thereby to remove him from the scene. Even if Willems' condescending attitude toward him may have disposed Almayer to welcome a change, Vinck's hints that Lingard is the wealthier man is the more effective bait. Willems, experienced and shrewd as he is, requires tougher handling. By his embezzlement of the master's money, he provides his rival not only with the desired weapon, but also with a shield of self-righteousness behind which that man hides his own dishonesties, for Vinck's early remark that Willems becomes dangerous because he knows too much, which is made under the pretense of "loyal criticism" (10), smacks of self-protective concerns. Conrad's presentation of Hudig, whose business transactions with Lingard resemble a "fight of two mastiffs" in Almayer's memory, shows him perfectly capable of protecting his own interests. When the narrator of *Almayer's Folly* communicates that Hudig has gone bankrupt, the early impression reemerges that Vinck's loyalty to the bank might bear some looking into, and the question invites itself to what degree the collapse of the bank may be the consequence of the cashier's untrustworthiness.

In this way, the later reappearance of the Vincks in Singapore is less of an inconsistency than Professor Gordan sees in it (52). On the contrary, their financial well-being, which allows them to have their daughters educated in Europe, and their standing in the society of Singapore, to which Mrs Vinck's snobbishness bears witness, strongly suggest that they have gained by Hudig's loss. There is also much consistency in the role of Mrs Vinck, who destroys Nina's relation with the white society of Singapore, and that of Mr Vinck, who earlier functions as an evil star in the lives of Almayer and Willems.

In an early letter to Mme Poradowska, Conrad asked whether fiction could be made interesting without the involvement of women (Cl I 171). The question is of interest inasmuch as it reflects the author's concern to make his fiction acceptable to the readers and thereby enables us to estimate the courage he mustered in producing "The Nigger of the 'Narcissus'." But it is even more interesting by the mere fact of having been raised since it gives away the author's reluctance to occupy himself with the creation of female characters. When Conrad nevertheless yielded to what appeared to him an artistic necessity, he resorted to the compromise solution of female characters who by origin and social status exist on the margin of their society. Ironically, however, it is precisely by their marginalization that they comment on that society and on Conrad's creative work.

Joanna da Souza, a half-caste issue of Hudig's moral licentiousness, is described as an accumulation of unattractive qualities. To her, marriage to a Dutchman means a raise in social status, and Willems is easily manipulated into marrying her because of the gain it brings him—a house and a secure career based on Hudig's favor. What the East in general is to Willems as a representative of white colonizers, that Joanna is in particular: undesired in herself, she becomes desirable on the basis of economic considerations.

The parallel situation of Joanna's role in her marriage to Willems and that of the colonial territory and population in relation to the Europeans present in it is obvious and consistent. Willems' first and lasting impression of his wife is one of untidiness and sloth. On a large scale, the white men register squalor, dirt, and inertia as prevailing characteristics in the colonial setting. The husband experiences Joanna as a weight around his neck just as the Europeans feel the burden of what, to them, are deprivations in the overseas territory. In both cases a necessary evil is endured for the sake of material profit, and as Willems welcomes an opportunity to get rid of Joanna, so the goal of the Europeans is to enjoy comfort and ease in their native country after an accumulation of wealth abroad.

Inferior intellectual capacity is an agreed-upon fact for Willems and the white colonizers in the case of Joanna as of all indigenous people. On it they found their sense of superiority and mission, and by it they justify their condescending, paternalizing attitude and the expectation to be applauded as liberators and redeemers. Despite his contempt for his wife, Willems sees himself bound in duty to care for her; and so does Lingard whose patronizing instincts overrule even Hudig, the woman's father, when he takes Joanna to Sambir to be reunited with her husband. Her actual helplessness and doubtful motivation in marrying the white man, like the tribal rivalries and disorders among the indigenous people which encourage interference from abroad, may invite the question to what degree they should account for the superior self-image of the colonizers.

For, vanity is one of the vices that thrive on the conditions Europeans find in the colonial setting. Lingard's modesty and actual achievements readily provide him with a willing audience to gratify it. But Willems has to resort to mental violence to force the attention of his wife. Her initial, vain attempt to resist and the subsequent dumb compliance with her husband's demands are small-scale reenactments of the violence done to the Malays at which Babalatchi's quotation of a white oppressor points: "Obey me and be happy, or die!" (226); these are the words he puts in the mouth of Lingard, the vanquisher of Omar. His pretense of humble subservience to Lingard, like Joanna's scared look, witnesses to the strangulation their spirit and personalities suffer from the white men's need to gratify their own ego.

Wherever Joanna appears, her lean arms clutch her child, Willems' son, for whom he shows hardly less disgust than for the mother and whom he readily abandons to her without scruples or second thoughts. She bears her burden in silent acceptance until the day of her husband's humiliation, when her concealed feelings of hatred and scorn break forth like a wild torrent. The act of dropping her child in a chair before she gives vent to her pent-up emotions is of symbolic significance since with her physical burden she temporarily sheds the fear and inhibitions that have made her the shiftless target of her husband's victimization.

Like a tempest, her self-assurance, sprung from the awareness of a lack in her husband, is soon spent, and what follows is even more demeaning than her former self-abasing attitude. When she expresses remorse, it may seem to be the consequence of Lingard's moralizing interference, as on the surface it actually is. Its roots, however, reach into the causes that, some years earlier, have made marriage to a white man appear desirable to Joanna and her clan. Willems' aberrations do not annul the qualities that make him superior in her eyes—as in his own—and on Joanna's scale of values the security and status that come with being the wife of a European outweigh the abuse and humiliations with which she pays for them. Joanna's situation parallels that of the leaders of Sambir who rid themselves of what they consider a white oppressor by bringing an Arab trader into the settlement, only afterwards to hoist the Dutch flag because under it is safety.

Despite his sustained presentation of Joanna as unattractive and inferior, the author gives her role an unexpected turn when she becomes the potential deliverer of her husband from captivity. Here, she, the unintelligent, slothful, weak, and guilt-stricken woman, controls the means that give access to all that is desirable to Willems. She summons the courage and moral strength to thwart Lingard's plan, to undertake a nightly journey with questionable individuals to an unknown destination, to confront her husband despite her sense of guilt, and to dare life with him once more. She possesses what, by his frenzy to get hold of the revolver, Willems admits is lacking in himself.

This inversion of roles is significant from the aspect of Conrad's view on women and on the question of colonialism. It gives the lie to the superiority, strength, and cleverness of which the male has prided himself all along, and it allows that to surface which in the female is denied by the marginalized existence that the author has assigned to her. This duality of meanings inherent in Joanna's role fully corresponds with the contradictory opinions which, in speaking about women, Conrad occasionally expressed. In consequence, one may be induced to wonder whether the implications of Joanna's life are consciously aimed at or whether they result from the strength of Conrad's creative vision which the author acknowledges at work in him, saying, "It isn't in me to improve what has got itself written" (CL I 48) and which, as implied here, is not fully controlled by his reasoning faculty.

In either case Joanna's function as a reflection of the larger context is undeniable. As the novel closes, the Europeans in Sambir are no longer of any consequence; knowing the Dutch governor in a safe distance, those who earlier felt oppressed by Lingard's heavy hand control the events on the Pantai river and, although the future remains uncertain for both Joanna and Lakamba's party, her safety lies in returning to her clan, as theirs consists in hanging together.

The understanding regarding both issues—imperialism and the author's view on women—which is gained from the study of Joanna's presence in the novel is substantiated and expanded by that of Aïssa. Being beautiful, strong, alert, and aggressive, she is a contrast to Joanna in most respects. But she likewise derives from mixed parentage, and having a fugitive pirate as her father, her existence is even more on the margin of society than that of Willems' wife. Even so, next to Babalatchi, Aïssa is the most outspoken critic of the West and its imperialistic ambitions, and through her Conrad points out the injustice of double standards for men and women much like a present-day advocate of women's rights.

Strength of heart, mind, and body is Aïssa's most obvious quality. Her fearless confrontation with danger and death and her unflinching filial piety earn her the narrator's comparison to the Trojan hero Aeneas. Tribal and personal history have taught Aïssa to trust in strength and since, in the eyes of the vanquished pirates, white men are the embodiment of strength, Willems' infatuation affects her as a political victory over him. This explains her fierce determination to retain her power over Willems and the sense of frustration when she discovers his weakness. Aïssa's giving of herself is of a political nature not only because she is used as a bait by Babalatchi. It is more so because her goal to keep Willems within the realm of her own world means to her a defeat of the West in which she sees her most threatening enemy. In a letter to Garnett, Conrad explained the inner battle of Aïssa and Willems as originating in a sense of loss "of things precious" to Willems when his passion has passed:

> Consequently—his deliberate effort to recall the passion as a last resort, as the last refuge of his regrets, from the obsession of his longing to return whence he came. It's an impulse of thought not of the senses. The senses are done with. Nothing lasts! So with Aïssa. Her passion is burnt out too. There is in her that desire to be something for him—to be in his mind in his heart— to shelter him in her affection—her woman's affection which is simply the ambition to be an important factor in another's life. They both long to have a significance in the order of nature or of society. To me they are typical of mankind where every individual wishes to assert his power, woman by sentiment, man by achievement of some sort—mostly base. (CL I 247)

Aïssa's hidden battle against the hold Europe has on Willems is one against the effects of its civilization. She diagnoses the problem correctly that confronts her relation with the white man. While she knows that her own strength derives from being untouched by that civilization, she also senses the barrier which this fact erects between herself and her lover. Even in his most exalted moments, Willems remains conscious of the degradation which his passion for the indigenous woman means and of the abyss that exists between them. Despite his infatuation, Willems never ceases to think of Aïssa as a "mere savage."

As in the previous novel, 'savage' is a frequently used word also in *An Outcast of the Islands*. There the person most often modified by it is Mrs Almayer; here it is Aïssa. In ten out of twenty-three cases the word refers to her and half of these are Willems' choices of it in thinking and speaking about Aïssa. This suggests that the basic meaning in Conrad's use of 'savage' denotes the opposite of being civilized. But since a wide range of possible nuances is inherent also in the meaning of the latter word, a look at a variety of examples is necessary to determine the prevailing one.

These show that 'savage' expresses both physical and mental states of Europeans as well as of Malays. In the case of the Rajah of Goak, who uses a gilt glass coach for a hen coop (8), of the "ill-behaved savage" Mahmat (316), and possibly also in that of the people with whom Willems compares his empty existence in Sambir (65), the word implies an absence of the external refinements of civilized behavior. When Willems and Almayer speak of Lakamba, Babalatchi, and the people under their influence as 'savages' (126, 128, 207, 274), the word is laden with disdain for the racially inferior which, in Mannoni's words, is "the European's over-compensation for an inferiority complex" (118). At times, 'savage' expresses a state of extreme emotions of white and indigenous characters (65, 249, 338, 358), and with reference to Europeans it occasionally serves as an invective (28, 205, 341). Most frequently, however, and in nearly all instances when it is applied to Aïssa, the word means a total absence of the physical and mental changes that result from exposure to and assimilation of civilizing influences (80, 91, 127, 156, 250, 269, 271, 300, 367).

The insights gained in this way confirm the conclusion to which *Almayer's Folly* has led. 'Savage' as used by Conrad has less to do with racial differences than with character, and more often than not, it is intended to reveal the speaker as much as the person to whom the word is applied. In light of his role as a weak, empty individual, Willems' frequent use of 'savage' and simultaneous emphasis on his own superiority as a civilized being are greatly ironic. He says in effect that civilization has taken from him that from which Aïssa derives her fierce strength.

If Willems, like Almayer, illustrates the Darwinian idea that in the process of becoming civilized humans lose vital power, Aïssa must be understood as the voice of that which has been lost to them. Therein lies the weightiness of her repeated accusations that Europe is a "land of lies and of evil from which nothing but misfortune ever comes" (144). With these words, Conrad makes her respond to the rhetorical question of Sir James Brooke, "Is it not sad to think that kingdoms are laid low, and the inhabitants oppressed and dispersed, whenever they come within the grasp of European civilization?" (Keppel 12). Brooke could write this because sincere concern had enabled him to divest himself of the prejudices of his own world in order to enter that of the colonial people. With this agreement between Aïssa, the voice of the uncivilized natives, and a colonial authority, Conrad best proves his freedom from racist intentions in his use of 'savage.'

As Aïssa unrelentingly points out the oppression her people suffer from the Europeans, she also shows up the injustice done to women. She does so by the example of her own life, which she uses to criticize the double standards by which men judge. "What more have you done?" she demands of Lingard after she has enumerated the dangers she has faced and the hardships she has borne (246). For this Lingard is unprepared; and although in words he pays tribute to her prowess, her sex does not allow him to do so also in the treatment which he gives her.

Her insistence in speaking to Lingard that due consideration should be given to her achievements is in sharp contrast with the strict adherence to the rules of propriety for Moslem women which Aïssa displays towards Abdulla. The political bent in her conduct is obvious. Being diplomatically sensitive, she meets both men on their own grounds, and this secures her a degree of victory over them: from Abdulla, Willems is passed on to Lingard and to her. But the result to which this victory leads confirms her earlier words that from Europe evil comes to those who are not white. In her hands the product of Western civilization, the revolver, can only be destructive; her victory becomes her loss, her memory of hatred and affection for a white man, with whom she has had nothing in common, the sole content of her remaining life.

The sombre ending of the novel is the result of the consistency with which the laws of cause and effect assert themselves. In the human context, they become the law of solidarity which answers Almayer's string of questions about the sense of the things that have happened in Sambir. Natives and whites are affected by the ambitions and the "failure of judgment" of a few, and although the conclusion of the novel echoes the word 'hope,' the text does not support the promise the word seems to give. Lingard is old and tired, Babalatchi feels betrayed by Abdulla, as Almayer does by Willems, the two women are removed again to their hidden existence, and the population of Sambir is caught in the power struggle of Arab and Malay leaders.

Again it is intertextuality that can provide meaning for the novel's suggestive conclusion. It has been seen earlier that the hope Abdulla can offer is doubtful even though he is the most firmly established person in Sambir when *An Outcast* ends. Despite his importance he remains confined to a covert plot also in *Almayer's Folly*, and since his way of advancing himself is the diminution of others, little can be expected from him besides further gain for himself. But in Nina Almayer, still a child when *An Outcast* closes, life gives itself another chance. It is significant that it is Aïssa who preserves this life when Nina is in danger of drowning. There is hope in the turn this life takes in *Almayer's Folly* not only because in Nina's son life continues, but more so because by the choices she makes she overcomes the weakening and enslaving value systems of her father and his companions.

III THE "WAYSIDE QUAGMIRES"—
IMAGERY AND CHARACTERIZATION

Much of what has been said about Conrad's use of imagery in *Almayer's Folly* is applicable to *An Outcast of the Islands* as well. As in the first novel, the author draws heavily upon nature imagery to reveal the mental and psychological states of his characters and to create atmosphere. The consciousness that his strength as an artist was in being descriptive and his choice of a setting unfamiliar to his readers are part of the reason that prompted his reliance on the imagery he chose; another is the fact that *An Outcast* aims not so much at effects achieved by action as derived from reflection. Although it is true that Conrad had still to learn what to leave unwritten, especially as regards the handling of metaphoric language in his first novels, as it stands, the imagery of *An Outcast* is important and deserves the reader's attention.

Despite its weightiness, the covert plot is of little consequence regarding the choice of leading images. These are decided by the deficiency of the protagonist who, like Kurtz, is "hollow at the core," a quality which in the colonial setting of Sambir is given representative connotations. The opening sentence of the novel introduces the theme by way of a metaphor. Willems, we are told, has "stepped off the straight path of his peculiar honesty . . . into the wayside quagmires." With great economy the image concretizes the state of Willems as that of a pilgrim who lacks solidity of character. The element into which he has stepped off the path of virtue is treacherous and unreliable. There is no firmness underneath the superficial greenness; it offers no support and the morasses in which Willems finds himself very soon and which mess up the lives of those with whom he comes in contact effectively illustrate his own moral condition. Willems cannot be trusted, because the thin, superficial layer of virtue on which he builds his position in the society of Macassar merely covers up the quagmires of self-deception and the lack of solidity within himself. Allowing for a great many varieties of modifications, this image of a pleasing surface that conceals treachery and emptiness recurs throughout the novel.

This metaphoric image best expresses Willems' role in the novel and the way in which his character becomes worthy of our study in spite of his dishonesties and vainglorious behavior. Unlike the protagonist of *Almayer's Folly*, Willems understands the gap between his illusions of himself and the reality of his life. He lives on two levels; while he upholds his belief in his white-man integrity, he perceives and acknowledges the degeneration of which he is capable. He knows that the greenness of his pretensions coexists with the morasses that are covered by it. This psychological insight, which he counters with ingenious evasions, places Willems in the company of Falstaff and renders him interesting. It also allows for some amount of tension in Willems and justifies the author's choice of this character as the protagonist of *An Outcast*.

As suggested by the key metaphor, the deeper truths about the characters of *An Outcast* are made known by the settings in which we find them, as well as by the way in which they relate to those settings. In the opening chapter, Macassar and Willems' bungalow are the means and witnesses to his triumphs and his shame. They impress with the attractiveness and luxuriance of their gardens and growths. But behind these hide squalor and vice.

On an incomparably larger scale, the dazzling beauty of tropical vegetation around Sambir covers up the violence, treachery, and decay at work in the human realm, as in the world of plants. In different ways, Sambir is an opportunity in the eyes of all who seek it. For Lingard, it is a source of wealth and the object of his Arcadian dreams. For Almayer, Lakamba, and Abdulla, it is a means of personal enrichment and power. For Willems, it is a hiding place. However, built on malodorous mud with houses protruding over the dead water of the bank, the settlement functions as a counterpart to the quagmires of the initial metaphor. The geographical unhealthiness and political unreliability of the setting complement each other. Moral degeneracy flourishes in that jungle of intrigues and lawless aspirations and betrays what is hollow in the expectations of all characters.

The scene of the protagonist's first encounters with the indigenous woman is as striking as her beauty; but it also is known to be very unhealthy, and it visualizes Aïssa's being as Willems experiences it.

He sees the woman first through the effects of sunshine and shadow, which suggest tenderness and mystery, "the impalpable distinctness of a dream," "an apparition behind a transparent veil" (70). Direct exposure, however, reveals the untamed quality of her being which finds its equivalent in the fierce struggle for survival of the tropical growth. Her look is "hard, keen, and narrow, like the gleam of sharp steel." There is about her "the expression of a wild and resentful defiance" (71).

During the early stages of their acquaintance, the two lovers appear to each other calm and composed; they are in harmony with the trees that surround them—big, still and straight. Meanwhile, the intensity of aspiring growth and forbidding gloom underneath the sun-caressed tops of the trees parallels the emotional development to which they are subject and which baffles and frightens Willems in his waking moments. The Dantesque image of the drowning swimmer (81), in which the death sensation of depravity and danger climaxes, corresponds with the death-in-life metaphor of nature. When the passion which the woman's beauty has aroused in him is dissipated, Willems finds himself as much choked and appropriated by her as is the stifled growth in the dark shades by the power of the wilderness. He feels that the woman clings to him as the parasitic plants do to the trees.

Paradoxically, Willems' surrender to his passion is also a surrender to an even more total isolation. Before Willems meets Aïssa, he is physically isolated by the remoteness of Sambir and the confinement of the trading station; he is also morally isolated by Lingard's lack of perception and Almayer's rejection; emotionally and intellectually he is isolated by his own egotism and sense of white superiority. But in his infatuation for a woman with whom he has nothing in common, he experiences an isolation that touches the essence of his being. The clearing in which Lingard abandons him with its fallow rice field, deserted huts, and pathless surrounding mirrors Willems' condition appropriately.

His enslavement by Aïssa and those who use her occurs in Lakamba's clearing, where Lingard finally makes him a prisoner. Like the character of the man after whom it is named, the clearing is known to be especially treacherous and unhealthy. In its populated state, it is the setting in which Lakamba and Babalatchi are made known to the reader. The former impresses with his princely descent and the latter with his unconditional loyalty. But behind the pretenses of the surface hides unreliability. These men are as remote from the order by which the society of Sambir functions as is the clearing from that settlement. In its seclusion it is an ideal setting for secrecy and intrigue, and the poisonous growth

surrounding it is the natural counterpart to the poison of discontent and
envy that lingers in Lakamba's heart.

Babalatchi likens the giant trees of the forest, one of which dominates
the inhabited part of the clearing, to Sambir's population (225).
Protected by indifference and ignorance he believes them and himself
beyond the reach of colonial powers. In light of the theme of imperialism
the tree in Lakamba's clearing assumes a strongly ironic function.
Lingard warns Babalatchi that the axes that fell even big trees are the
product of white hands. In Willems' death, caused by a bullet that was
produced in a European factory, the West defeats itself. Meantime, the
tree that witnesses this defeat remains untouched. Although disillusioned
by the role Abdulla has assumed, Babalatchi, the master of Lakamba's
vaccillating mind, continues to scheme and in doing so to play with live
embers (122). The life of Lingard, on the contrary, is greatly changed.
He feels old and tired, and *Almayer's Folly* narrates his retirement from
Sambir while Babalatchi is still very active.

Aïssa's dual ethnic background contributes extensively to the
development of the imperial theme. In her, Arabs and Malays overcome
the white power not only by using her passion for Willems in order to
defeat Lingard, but even more by her own intrinsic being to the making
of which both have contributed. The accummulation of the number three
in connection with the events that surround Willems' betrayal of Lingard
assumes a symbolic function inasmuch as it suggests the triple force of
Arabs, Malays, and whites who contend for power in Sambir. Willems'
first encounter with Aïssa occurs after he has been in Sambir for three
months. She pressures him into the betrayal of Lingard's secret by
remaining inaccessible to him for three days. These days become a time
of anxiety and doubt for Babalatchi (98, 112), the cause of her father's
threefold curse on Willems (100), a period of helpless rage for the white
man (119), and a matter with which she taunts and threatens Willems
after their reunion (127, 140, 141 , 143). Finally, Abdulla appears on
the scene with an escort of three large canoes (113).

Despite his important role in the novel, Abdulla remains an elusive
character. He is distinctly seen physically, but his personality evades
clear recognition. It is said that in compliance with the teaching of
his religion he is devout, humble, generous, and charitable. But in
his conduct he proves himself hungry for power and wealth; he is
fiercely proud, ready for intrigues and hypocrisy, and prepared to back
up his ambitions with firearms. His restless wanderings from island to
island, before he finally settles down in Sambir, correspond with the
sense of uncertainty as to his character with which he leaves the reader.

Inasmuch as his function is largely confined to the extensive covert plot that connects *Almayer's Folly* with *An Outcast*, this indistinct view of Abdulla is functional. For, like the meshes of the net in which Willems and Lingard get caught, he achieves his successes by not being seen clearly, not even by Babalatchi.

Repeatedly the author uses spatial references to concretize the condition of the protagonist's mental state. The intoxication of his unexpected first encounter with Aïssa is rendered in terms of an enlarged, heightened perception of himself and his environment: "How changed everything seemed! The river was broader, the sky was higher. How fast the canoe flew under the strokes of his paddle! Since when had he acquired the strength of two men or more?" (72). His humiliation in Macassar and his betrayal of Lingard, on the other hand, he experiences as a diminution of self. The world has suddenly become vaster. "It seemed to him that the world was bigger, the night more vast and more black" (30) and Lingard is taller and more unapproachable (257).

As Willems' character is mainly visualized by deceitful land settings, so is that of Lingard mostly seen through associations with the sea, his ship *Flash*, and the Pantai river in its positive qualities. The wideness and depth of the sea correspond with the wide scope of Lingard's role in both overt and covert plot. On the sea, Lingard has established his reputation, and his craft is the paramount symbol of his good fortune (13), which deserts him when the ship is lost (199-200). With the discovery of the entrance to the river, he has become special. But when his secret about it is divulged, he is ordinary and unimportant. "His river! By it . . . he was interesting. This secret . . . was the greater part of his happiness, but he only knew it after its loss" (202). The cause of trouble which the river has become because of Willems' treachery is made concrete in the banality and bother of its flies and mosquitoes which plague the white men (169). Ironically, Lingard likened himself to a blue bottle fly when he chased after the disgraced Willems in Macassar to save him from his shame. It is the vain chase of such a fly that illustrates the depth into which his life has sunk and which he can no longer master when Willems has betrayed him (32, 169).

In addition to the function of the brig as a symbol of Lingard's good luck, there is much meaning in the fact that the loss of his prestige in Sambir occurs simultaneously with that of the ship. Considering his earlier words to Willems that the sea is the only place for an honest man (42), his recourse to treasure hunting, when he is landbound, is suggestive of the physical and moral deterioration of the Rajah Laut in consequence of these events. In a subtle manner, those words which

Lingard pronounces when he is about to take Willems to Sambir acquire prophetic meaning and implicate him in the act of betrayal of which Willems becomes guilty.

The Pantai river is as many-faceted as the surrounding jungle. It has been seen that to Lingard it is a "friendly" river as long as he can call it "his" (200). Willems finds its water as slimy and dirty as he himself feels when he has yielded to his desire for the native woman (73); meanwhile Babalatchi compares Willems' moral softness to that of its mud: "I knew he would be soft in my hand like the mud of the river," he tells Abdulla (119). It is characteristic of the old schemer that he recognizes the river's heartless, deadly, and imprisoning potential as well as its readiness to be submissive, to save, and to serve. Almayer, finally, sees in the river an image of life and in the dead log that drifts down to its grave in the sea human destinies (291).

The reappearance of Almayer in *An Outcast* invites the reader to appraise the protagonist of *Almayer's Folly* in perspective and to add substance to the flat image of him which the earlier novel offers. The picture remains the same insofar as Almayer is consistent in his egotistic preoccupation with a dream of wealth. But seeing him interact with Lingard and Willems at a time when his trust that he will attain his dream is still unchecked, adds to that picture the color of impudence, arrogance, and mental limitation. *An Outcast*, furthermore, enhances the understanding of Almayer in the earlier novel by filling in the sketchy background scenes—his initial relations with Willems and the early stages of Almayer's unhappy marriage.

The population of Sambir looks upon Almayer and Willems as representatives of Europe and their disruptive relationship has therefore public consequences. Added to Willems' disloyalty to Lingard, it is a weapon which Malays and Arabs turn against the white men themselves. Here, too, the image of a pleasing surface—their white skin—that hides morasses is applicable. It is significant that Almayer sees a network of vapors rather than gold bars as he watches the Pantai at sunset after Willems' betrayal has shocked him into a brief state of awareness of reality (291). What he sees is the network of causes and consequences in human relationships. But the mood is transitory and the lesson of the sky is lost on Almayer, because he remains centered on his selfish dream.

Almayer's presence in *An Outcast* also effects a clearer understanding of his relation to his daughter. In his possessive love of the child he contrasts drastically with Willems, who hardly acknowledges his son as his own. But the difference is only external since both are motivated by self-love; for in Nina, Almayer loves himself. The nightly scene of his visit to the sleeping child, which resembles idol worship (320), means therefore worship at the shrine of his self-centered ambitions and explains the steadying effect the child has on the father during the unrest in Sambir after Abdulla's arrival. This relationship is consistently developed in *Almayer's Folly* and objectified by the rocking chair that functions as Nina's cradle in *An Outcast*.

An Outcast is likewise enriched by the reappearance of the Chinese Jim-Eng who, on account of his opium addiction, has created a doubtful impression in *Almayer's Folly*. As if wanting to correct this, Lingard, a friend of the Chinese in general and of Jim-Eng in particular for having brought him to Sambir, speaks of him as a "first class" Chinese in this novel (181). There is consistency in the presentation of this character inasmuch as here, just as in the earlier novel, Jim-Eng dares to differ from the crowd of Sambir inhabitants. As he was the only one who befriended the white man in the extremity of his disillusionment in *Almayer's Folly*, so he is also alone in loyalty to the British flag and to Lingard when the Dutch one is hoisted in Sambir and Abdulla is established as the new trader of the settlement. From the aspect of imperialism and of Conrad's frequent choice of Chinese as minor characters of his fiction with eastern settings, it is an enlightening detail that can help to avoid misreadings. At the same time, Jim-Eng's development in Sambir from an active, fit business man to a drug addict increases the irony of Lingard's role in these novels, because in the Chinese Conrad presents another one of Lingard's doomed protégés, as Cedric Watts has pointed out (137).

In harmony with the symbolic effect achieved by settings is that of the forces of nature. As in *Almayer's Folly*, neither sun nor moon are indicative of comfort or benevolence. It is characteristic of the author's Schopenhauerian leanings that he generally diverges from the conventional use of light-darkness symbolism. Brightness is neither connotative of goodness nor of understanding. In addition to the dazzling effect of light that blinds Almayer to important details, sunlight suggests passion when Willems comes to warn Almayer in the noonday heat (85), and so does the moon when it is likened to a traveller who seeks rest with the lover (61).

Emphasis is put on the shadows created by light, the shadows in which the vegetation of the jungle rots, in which human depravity flourishes and which supports the protagonist's vain claim to achievement. In this context, the early scene of Willems hailing his shadow in a moonlight night (10) complements the image of the quagmires into which he has stepped. It attains its full ironic effect when seen in the perspective of Schopenhauer's philosophy, which leads to Plato. Since according to the latter only eternal ideas are real, the shadow, Willems' proud possession, is doubly removed from reality; and so are the assurance and self-affirmation that he derives from it.

As in the previous novel, the important, often shady events of the novel happen in the darkness of night. It is night when Lingard picks up the teenage Willems on the quay of Macassar and when he does so again fourteen years later. At night, Babalatchi and Lakamba hatch the plan for Lingard's destruction; Willems transacts his business with Abdulla; Lingard goes to mete out justice to his protégé; and Joanna sets out to rescue her husband. However, in darkness truth also asserts itself. Willems comes to recognize the gap between himself and Aïssa and with this his own lostness. In his nightly conversation with Babalatchi and Aïssa, Lingard arrives at an understanding of the motivation that has led to Willems' betrayal and of the tainted nature of his own relation to that man. Confronted with Willems, Abdulla learns facts about his white rivals which he had not guessed before. Finally, an approaching storm darkens the morning when Lingard pronounces his judgment on Willems, by which the latter is forced to recognize the truth that his acts do "interfere with the very nature of things" (3).

The storm is the summary metaphor of the ultimate ruin to which Willems' emptiness leads. It is the concretization of the "immense cataclysm of his disaster" (341). Significantly, it announces itself with the light of Aïssa's first smile (71); it is in preparation during the weeks of struggle and surrender; and it discharges itself with full force in the moment when Willems' surrogate father disowns his protégé (283).

However, the storm purges without effecting purification. With the departure of the father figure, the mother elements, water and earth, vie with each other to appropriate the man—not to invigorate and restore, but to erase and absorb him (284). The mother elements are destructive forces for Willems, because his egotism negates life. In this way, Almayer's association of the sea with a grave acquires prophetic significance and scope.

IV HOLLOWNESS VERSUS JUSTICE AND JUDGMENT— STRUCTURE AND NARRATIVE DEVICES

A good portion of *An Outcast of the Islands* was written before Conrad's first novel was published. The author neither knew how the reading public would respond to *Almayer's Folly*, nor could he consult the opinion of reviewers and critics while planning this second piece of fiction. Nevertheless, intuition told Conrad that his first novel was not likely to win him a large readership. It has been seen earlier that before the novel had reached its final stage of composition, it had made Conrad wonder whether its plot was clear enough and whether his narrative method was understandable. Prompted by his determination not to "live in an attic" (Garnett 9) and not to write for a coterie, he consciously aimed at simplicity and lucidity in writing *An Outcast of the Islands*. As a result, Conrad's second novel is less demanding in structure and time scheme than the previous one.

At first sight it appears that *An Outcast* is altogether structured on the basis of the role Willems plays as an exponent of European ambitions in a colonial setting. In parts one and two the lacking moral solidity of his character is demonstrated in a variety of ways and manifestations. Part three displays the immediate consequences that follow from it for Lingard and Almayer, and this gives rise to the idea of retribution in the mind of the Rajah Laut; the last two parts prepare for and finally show the punishment that Willems' conduct earns him.

With the introduction of the theme of retribution and justice, however, it becomes obvious that these additional themes also affect the novel's structure. Although moral emptiness remains an important issue in the later half of *An Outcast*, most of the time it has bearing on the action only indirectly. Furthermore, underlying the overt plot and frequently merging with its structure is suspended the web of the covert plot. It is introduced at the end of the fourth chapter of part one with Lingard's question "I wonder what it means" (45), which Abdulla's conspicuous greeting elicits from him, and it is consistently woven by the Arab trader and his clan, first with the assistance of Babalatchi and Lakamba and later with that of his nephew Reshid. For, far from being content with the gains he has obtained in *An Outcast*, Abdulla continues to scheme when the novel ends. Though covert for long stretches, it is this underlying structure of Abdulla's contention with Lingard that provides an additional dimension for much of what happens in Willems' story and thereby renders the treatment of the theme of imperialism in this novel complex and colorful.

The novel's division into five parts—comparable to a Shakespearean drama—enabled the author to balance the two themes that dominate the overt plot against each other. He did so by assigning a nearly equal number of pages to the treatment of each. Parts four and five, which center on the problematic theme of justice, are of the same length as parts one and two, which concentrate on the theme of moral emptiness. Lingard, who feels called to help justice assert itself, moves from a peripheral position into the center of action by becoming its bearer in part four. Thus the duality of themes that decide the main action prepares for a duplication of climactic experiences.

Looking at the individual parts of the novel with their unequal number of chapters and pages, a pattern of development emerges which shows a gradual decrease in movement and events from the end of part two through part four. The last part once more offers a slight stir of action. But the decisive moments—Willems' ultimate recognition of the "immense cataclysm of his disaster" and the ironic expansion of his existence in his death—are characterized by silence and immobility.

Part one promises swift movement and a comparative wealth of information. Starting in *medias res* and using flashbacks, the author acquaints his reader in three introductory chapters with the protagonist's background, his relation to Lingard, his success, and the fall that brings him to the contemplation of suicide. In chapters four to seven, complication builds up. By taking Willems to Sambir, Lingard provides the young man with the eagerly desired secret of the navigatibility of the Pantai river and the inimical Malay elements in Sambir with a tool for his own destruction. Almayer, Lingard's second protégé, readily assists in the process by isolating Willems on account of his own jealousy. Part one ends with Willems' hopeless infatuation with the native woman Aïssa.

The following part develops the Malays' intrigue against Lingard. Conveniently they use Willems, who has become a helpless slave of passion, and Abdulla, whose interests for the time being coincide with their own. With Willems' agreement to pilot the Arab trader into the river, the climax of action is achieved at the end of the novel's first third. To strengthen its effect, the last chapter of part two demonstrates the lost state of the protagonist in the hands of the indigenous woman.

Much of the remaining two thirds is given to Lingard's attempt to comprehend the motivation underlying the behavior of Willems and to that man's mental experience of the depth into which he has sunk. Since in both cases the author is concerned with mental and emotional states there is neither need nor room for activity. The length to which the novel develops in this part frequently meets with the objection of readers and critics. Considering, however, that it is meant to reflect Lingard's difficulty to arrive at an understanding of his own relation to Willems and of that man's motivation in betraying him, there is justification at least for part of it.

In part three, which functions as a fulcrum balancing the two halves of the novel, Almayer enters as the narrator of the events that have changed life in Sambir. Resourceful as ever, Lingard outlines a future for himself, Almayer, and Nina in mining for gold. But the narrator's lengthy reflection on Lingard's personality, on which part three ends, leaves the reader with a strong sense of the consternation and perplexity that Willems' treachery causes the Rajah Laut. To obtain some help in his search for light in this matter, Lingard spends a night conversing with Babalatchi, whom he had not intended to visit. After that, in chapter three, he listens at length to a demonstration of Aïssa's sentiments, although originally he had no mind to speak to her. In the meantime Willems remains invisible.

The night spent in this way is not wasted, because Lingard gains two important insights. First, he recognizes something in himself that has to do with Willems' conduct; he calls it an "error of judgment." Second, he comes to the recogniton of passion for a woman he now hates as the cause of Willems' loss of freedom and self-esteem. In this way, Lingard's mind becomes clear: he will rid himself of his mistake by abandoning Willems to the cause and object of his depravity, Aïssa. When in the following chapter Willems finally appears on the scene and Lingard exhorts him to explain himself, there is nothing for the latter to say. The anti-climax, which consists in Lingard's sentence over Willems and his subsequent abandonment of his protégé, now turned his shame, is therefore appropriately marked by the silence and inactivity of a deserted clearing. Doubly so, because with Lingard's resolution to withhold mercy and compassion from Willems in the future, hopelessness stifles life in all its manifestations. The psychological tension among the three characters in Lakamba's clearing is reflected in the storm that is building up during this final disruption of relationships.

The concluding part of *An Outcast* puts the theme of justice within a wider frame of treatment by adding the perspective of human solidarity. Since most other themes are closely connected with it, all are brought together in the final chapters. For a brief period, the farcical role Almayer plays in the first chapters of part five causes some movement once more. But the decisive happenings—Willems' ultimate recognition of the "immense cataclysm of his disaster" and the ironic expansion of his existence in the moment of his death—are again characterized by the silence and immobility that surround them.

If attention to tone and atmosphere is an important aspect of Conrad's narrative approach to *An Outcast*, the attempt to make Willems psychologically convincing is a more significant one. To the degree that Conrad succeeds in this effort, *An Outcast* exceeds the creative achievement of *Almayer's Folly*, even though the stylistic weaknesses of the second novel—lack of subtlety, crowding of modifiers, heavy use of nature imagery, in addition to the ponderous motion of the narrative—interfere more with the enjoyment of reading than in the previous one. Much of the appeal of *An Outcast* depends on the effect of the psychological make-up of the protagonist when he consistently sustains his superior self-image even while he faces the reality of his degradation, for the critical situations that bring Willems face to face with the latter prove only to the reader that there is a discrepancy between Willems' intellectual capacity and moral inadequacy. To the protagonist, they are opportunities to reassure himself of his singular value by finding the cause of evil outside his own being.

At times this confrontation of the protagonist with the truths about himself is brought about in dramatic scenes; more often it is achieved by frequent shifts from an omniscient point of view to Willems' own. The latter method enables the author to demonstrate Willems' skill in detaching himself mentally from his moral and emotional being and in making his consistent disclaimer for his deeds plausible. As Willems sees it, the madness that caused him to embezzle Hudig's money and the enslavement by passion that made him betray his white identity and Lingard's trading interests are extrinsic to his personality; they are factors for which Providence is responsible. The self-laudatory attitude with which Willems invariably presents himself when he is confronted with the facts of his wrong-doing might smack of melodrama were it not for the effort with which Conrad aims at showing the protagonist from his interiority.

In gifting Willems with adeptness at objectifying his defects, the author achieves some complexity of effect. Inasmuch as Willems protects the illusion of himself by establishing a correlation between his own guilty actions and the fallen state of the world around him, he integrates himself into it without intending to do so. Conrad's narrative scheme prepares for this from the beginning when simultaneously with the protagonist's hollowness he makes known the corruptions of those who judge him— their jealousies, infidelities, debaucheries, treacheries, and intrigues. In the others' actual faults, the protagonist finds the desired support for his escapist attitude. When he feels for his enemies "all the hate of his race, of his morality, of his intelligence" (126), he is therefore hardly more hypocritical and self-righteous than they are.

The narrative effect of the mental dodges which Willems performs is enhanced by Conrad's skillful handling of time elements. Although he makes frequent use of chance and coincidence for the shaping of human destinies, his goal is to be realistic. To this end, he provides regular information on the passage of time. The observation that Almayer's watch is going only when Lingard is in Sambir is of interest, because it not only illustrates how much Almayer is out of touch with the reality of his existence. It also suggests the older man's function as a corrective to Almayer's unrealistic expectations towards life.

In general the time scheme is clearer in this novel than in *Almayer's Folly*. Again it is the successful manipulation of retrospective narrative that provides most of the opportunities for suspense and discoveries, and flashbacks are employed not only to establish the background for plot and character, but also to achieve some degree of intensity of narration.

At a second reading, this is increased by the effects of dramatic irony. The Lingard-Willems relationship, above all, becomes poignant in this way, for instance, when Lingard tells Willems, "I have no doubt my secret will be safe with you" (43), and, "I shall keep the venomous breed out, if it costs my fortune" (45). But Conrad's view on imperialism reveals itself mainly by the irony that results from the combined effect of overt and covert plot. Lingard's "bitter wish for complete justice" (229), of which Babalatchi says that it is the only thing left to the natives after the Europeans have invaded their territories (229), finds fulfillment in a way vastly different from what the Rajah Laut had imagined and desired. To discover this larger dimension, however, and with it the merit of its narrative art, *An Outcast* presupposes a reader who is willing to allow for its imperfections and who does not approach it as an adventure story.

THE RESCUE

I THE GESTATION OF *THE RESCUE*

More than any other work, the third part of the Lingard trilogy tested Conrad's calling as an artist. It appears that in conception the novel was completed within less than two years, for when in September 1897 the author corresponded with William Blackwood of the reputed *Blackwood's Edinburgh Magazine*, he gave a clear outline of the story and its underlying ideas (CL I 381). The greater part of Conrad's career as a novelist, however, was to pass before he was able to give literary expression to his mental construct.

Conrad's attempt to write this sequel of his trilogy did not follow right after the completion of *An Outcast of the Islands*. First he turned to an altogether different subject, *The Sisters*, which was to be the story of a young Ukrainian artist living in Passy, Paris, and a Basque girl. Zdislav Najder suggests that Conrad's choice of this subject and its setting had its roots in the author's relationship with Mme Poradowska who lived in Passy and in whose stories Ukrainian motifs are frequent (182-3).

Whatever Conrad's reasons may have been for trying himself at materials that had nothing in common with those labelled "exotic" by his readers and critics, the attempt was a failure. At the advice of E. Garnett, Conrad abandoned the fragment when he had finished about thirty-five printed pages (Najder 187-8). From it he returned to the Bornean setting and the familiar character of Tom Lingard.

He took these steps in March 1896, the month which brought the publication of *An Outcast* (March 4) and his wedding to Jessie E. George (March 24). The crowding of these important events in the same month is striking and suggests that they influenced each other. If Conrad derived his stimuli for writing *The Sisters* from his relationship with Mme Poradowska, they were certainly diminished with his—in the eyes of his friends—precipitated marriage. In proportion to it, his interest in the themes and settings of his Malay novels was invigorated with the publication of *An Outcast*. In letters to E. Garnett and E.L. Sanderson, written toward the end of the month, Conrad referred to conversations in which he had presented his plans for what he called a "sea-story," and he announced its title as *The Rescuer: A Tale of Narrow Waters* (CL I 268-70).

On Ile-Grande in Brittany, where the newlyweds had rented a cottage, Conrad began writing the new book. He was confident that he would finish it within a year, and the pace at which he progressed at the beginning justified his optimism. On April 13, 1896, he mailed the first twenty-four pages of *The Rescuer* to Garnett. But the mere act of doing so betrays the insecurity and doubts that plagued him. "I am so afraid of myself, of my likes and dislikes, of my thought and of my expression, that I must fly to You . . . for anything to kill doubt with. . . . Is the thing tolerable? Is the thing readable?" (CL I 273) he wrote in the accompanying letter. Garnett's answer was strongly encouraging: "Excellent, oh Conrad. Excellent. I have read every word of *The Rescuer* and think you have struck a new note. The opening chapter is most artistic; just what is right for an opening chapter. The situation grips one with great force. It is as clearly and forcibly *seen* as if one had spent a month on those seas." "Had I suspected the long Odyssey of acute distress and worry that Conrad was to undergo over *The Rescuer* . . . I would, cf course, have persuaded him to abandon the book," Garnett later reflected on that matter (Garnett 18-19). A letter to E.L. Sanderson which Conrad sent a day after he had mailed the manuscript to Garnett would suggest that Conrad had posted it only for the purpose of arranging for the publication of his new novel. "I want Unwin to have a sample to show the Mag: Editors," he wrote to his friend (CL I 274).

Neither his concentrated interest in the subject nor the energy with which he had approached this project lasted. Very soon the first interruptions ocurred: Conrad fell ill and after his recovery he composed "The Idiots," a short story of ten thousand words on Breton peasant life. He finished it on May 22, and writing to his publisher T. Fisher Unwin on that day, he mentioned that *The Rescuer* had grown to twenty thousand words and that "for fear of doing badly" due to ill health he had not been working on it recently (CL I 279). "I have about 70 pages of that most rotten twaddle," he remarked in a letter to Garnett on the same day (CL I 281). One might be inclined to take his words as another example of his habitual depreciation of the things for which he cared.

There are lines in that letter, however, which strongly suggest that Conrad was actually groping in the dark. What is more, they offer a clue to the nature of the difficulties that plagued him. "Something brings the impression off—makes its effect. What? It can be nothing but the expression—the arrangement of words, the style—Ergo: the style is not dishonourable" (CL I 281). Although they were written in reference to H.G. Wells's review of *An Outcast*, these words echo the lines which Conrad had sent with his first twenty-four pages of *The Rescuer* on April 13: "I am afraid . . . of my expression . . ." The words of the reviewer aggravated the sense of helplessness which increasingly took hold of Conrad as he tried to write *The Rescuer*. He was sensitive to his critic precisely because of his frustrating struggle to develop a style that could satisfy both his readers and his own creative conscience. Complaints referring to this specific problem recur in Conrad's correspondence throughout the years during which he was working on this novel. Despite his exhausting efforts, he only achieved results that numbed him.

He forged ahead all the same and on June 2, 1896, he wrote: ". . . every day The Rescuer crawls a page forward—sometimes in cold despair—at times with hot hope. I have long fits of depression, that in a lunatic asylum would be called madness" (CL I 284). A few days later he finished the first part and mailed it to Garnett on June 10. In the letter that accompanied the manuscript he voiced all the doubts that had been part of his creative work since the time he had started to write as a professional. He worried about his readership: "will anybody . . . have the patience to read such twaddle"? He doubted the structure and style of his writing: "Here I have used up 103 pages of manuscript to relate the events of 12 hours. I have done it in pursuance of a plan. But is the plan utterly wrong? Is the writing utter bosh?" Worst of all, Conrad doubted his conception of the new novel, the "sincerity of [his] own impressions" (CL I 286-7).

In light of the emphasis which throughout his career as a writer Conrad put on fidelity to his sensations, the admission that he was not sure of the sincerity of his impressions is significant. The explanation he offered to Garnett a week later saying that the impressions and sensations he has had in earlier days have faded touches only the surface of his trouble (CL I 289). The real reason of the author's sentiment of being insincere derived from his attempt to do something that went counter to his understanding of the way that leads to success in creative writing and thus was an infidelity to his calling as an artist.

When in 1895 Conrad expounded his theory on this matter to Noble, he wrote:

You must treat events only as illustrative of human sensation—
as the outward sign of inward feelings—of live feelings—
which alone are truly pathetic and interesting. You have much
imagination; . . . Well, that imagination (I wished I had
it!) should be used to create human souls; to disclose human
hearts—and not to create events that are properly speaking
accidents only. To accomplish it you must . . . give yourself up
to your emotions . . . you must squeeze out of yourself every
sensation, every thought, every image—mercilessly, without
reserve and without remorse; you must search the darkest
corners of your heart, the most remote recesses of your brain;—
you must search them for the image, for the glamour, for the
right expression. And you must do it sincerely, at any cost; You
must do it so that at the end of your day's work you should feel
exhausted, emptied of every sensation and every thought, with
a blank mind and an aching heart, with the notion that there is
nothing—nothing left in you. To me it seems that this is the
only way to achieve true distinction—or even to go some way
towards it. (CL I 252)

"When I speak about writing from an inward point of view," he explained
five days later, "I mean from the depth of Your own inwardness" (CL I
253). The above letter is quoted at such length, because it bears witness
to the degree to which in writing *The Rescuer* Conrad was willing to
diverge from the convictions expressed in this document.

He did so in response to a well-meant advice of Garnett who, contrary
to an earlier one in which he had admonished Conrad "to follow his
own path" (Garnett 9), had made Conrad conscious of the reader's
expectations towards him: "Am I mindful enough of Your teaching—
of Your expoundings of the ways of the reader?" (CL I 273) Conrad
asked him in the letter that accompanied the first sample of *The Rescue*.
Earlier, when he had decided to add a sequel to his first two novels, he
wrote to his friend, "It will be on the lines indicated to you. I surrender
to the infamous spirit which you have awakened within me and as I want
my abasement to be very complete I am looking for a sensational title.
You had better help O Gentle and Murderous Spirit!" (CL I 268).

With the decision to write a novel that centered on a "gentleman and
a lady cut out according to the regulation pattern" (LL I 164n1) and
to make it "a kind of glorified book for boys" (CL I 392), Conrad put
stumbling blocks in his own way. He soon realized that he could not
attain these goals by following his creative intuition without producing

a "strange and repulsive hybrid" (CL I 296). Instead of writing from the depth of his "own inwardness," Conrad had to search for the "right expression" beyond himself.

Since in conception and execution Conrad had made himself dependent on the opinion of others, he had no point of reference to judge his own writing. It left him with the undefined feeling that he could not "believe in the book" (CL I 288). He strove to keep up the "new note" which Garnett had applauded in the first sample of *The Rescuer*, but he wrote with increasing diffidence. Thus he ended the letter that accompanied the completed first part of *The Rescuer* on the way to Garnett with the prediction that he would probably discontinue writing till he heard from his friend (CL I 287).

Conrad did attempt to write before he received the expected response, but the result was more frustrating than ever. There is little reason to disbelieve him when he says that in nine days he could finish only one page. "Now I've got all my people together I don't know what to do with them. The progressive episodes of the story *will* not emerge from the chaos of my sensations. I feel nothing clearly" (CL I 288).

The insecurity that characterized Conrad's work on *The Rescuer* from the beginning bears witness to the fact that Conrad's difficulties derived not only and not in the first place from the romantic relationship between Captain Lingard and Edith Travers which he was to establish. Even before he was faced with this task, his problems seemed insurmountable. Not so much his choice of an "uncongenial subject" but the reasons for that choice were the root of Conrad's troubles. Although it is true that Garnett contributed essentially to the making of the novelist Joseph Conrad, it is also evident that in the case of *The Rescuer* the author's dependence on the opinion of that friend had a stifling effect on his creative vision.

The shorter fiction which Conrad produced during those months of struggle with *The Rescuer* prove that he did have much power of imagination and expression. Two magazines, the *Cornhill* and the *Cosmopolis*, had rejected "The Idiots," but had invited Conrad to send shorter stories for publication (CL I 286, 292). Aside from financial considerations, Conrad's reason for writing short fiction was the need to balance the strain which *The Rescuer* caused him. On July 22, 1896, he surprised Garnett with the first of what he intended to become a volume of shorter pieces. "I am pleased with it. That's why you shall get it" (CL I 292), he wrote.

The piece to which Conrad referred was "An Outpost of Progress." Its composition had allowed the author to draw from personal experiences

in the Congo. He had also continued to treat themes that had occupied
him in the writing of his first two novels and that were not absent from
The Rescuer: colonialism, racism, and the doubtful ethical foundations of
western civilization. In letters to Unwin and Garnett, Conrad expressed
the satisfaction which he had derived from writing the story; he was
pleased with the result of his effort. Characteristically, however, in
writing to Garnett he resumed the tone of insecurity in the same breath
as he expressed his belief in the piece's artistic value. In the following
weeks, while still in Brittany, Conrad wrote "The Lagoon" and part of
The Nigger of the 'Narcissus' (CL I 296, 308n3).

He also continued to struggle with *The Rescuer*. On July 10, he sent
an optimistic report to Garnett: "I am now setting Beatrix, her husband
and Linares (the Spanish gent) on their feet. It's a hell of a job—as
Carter would say. However I trust you will find that they stand firmly
on their pins when I am done with them. I am trying to make all that
short and forcible. I am in a hurry to start and raise the devil generally
upon the sea" (CL I 291).

The hurry was of brief duration. Twelve days later, Conrad admitted:
"There is very little more of Rescuer written" (CL I 292); and by
August 5, he suffered from a severe depression that made continuation
seem impossible. "I begin to fear that I have not enough imagination—
not enough power to make anything out of the situation; That I cannot
invent an illuminating episode that would set in a clear light the persons
and feelings. I am in desperation and I have practically given up the
book" (CL I 296). When he wrote to the publisher four days later, he
explained the situation differently: "The short story like a fell disease
got me under—and the *Rescuer* has to wait. But I am thinking of him
and perhaps he will be all the better for it in the long run" (CL I 298).

It did have to wait. On August 14, Conrad confided to Garnett, "I wish
I could tackle the *Rescuer* again. I simply *can't!*" (CL I 301). At the
end of September, the Conrads returned to England (Najder 536n28) and
when the author mentioned the novel again, on November 13, it was—
surprisingly enough—for the purpose of communicating negotiations for
its publication. After a disagreement with T. Fisher Unwin, the publisher
he took into consideration was the House of Smith Elder. "I have
just returned from my interview with Mr Reginald Smith," he wrote
to Garnett,

> and, having heard his proposals, seek your advice. He began the
> conversation by asking how long it would take me to finish the
> *Rescuer*. I replied: six months or so. Then he said that . . . the

offer should be made after the book was finished. He put a
stress on that. . . . Then I spoke about the serial of *Rescuer*.
There also he did not say anything definite. . . . I feel horribly
unsettled. It takes the savour out of the work. And the "N" is
not yet quite finished. Then to go on toiling over the *Rescuer*
without knowing anything about a reward is distasteful. (CL I
315-6)

Nothing came of those negotiations, but on December 7 Conrad was in
a rare mood of exhilaration. He had succeeded in getting W.E. Henley,
editor of the *New Review*, interested in *The Nigger of the 'Narcissus.'* "I
will drink to the success of the *Rescuer*," he wrote in a note to Garnett,
whom he planned to meet in London (CL I 323). In the following
weeks, Conrad was intensely occupied with finishing *The Nigger* and in
the middle of January 1897, the task of writing was accomplished (CL
I 332n1); proofreading and revisions occupied some of his time as late
as October of the same year (CL I 395).

Even after the completion of *The Nigger*, Conrad did not return to *The
Rescuer*. On February 7, he mentioned another short piece, "Karain,"
which he planned to write in order to include it in the first volume of
short stories that was to be published by Unwin. "The *Rescuer* sleeps
yet the sleep of death. Will there be a miracle and a resurrection? Quien
sabe!" (CL I 338), he concluded the note.

The miracle did not happen at the completion of "Karain." Instead
Conrad began to write "The Return," a story which required much more
time and energy than he originally had allotted for it and which brought
him no satisfaction when he was done with it (CL I 386). He responded
to Garnett's comment on that story with the significant observation "it
is evident that my fate is to be descriptive and descriptive only. There
are things I *must* leave alone" (CL I 387). This self-appraisal explains
much of the distress *The Rescuer* caused Conrad. He had reached that
point of the story's development at which he was to confront the main
characters with each other. He could neither trust to achieve the task
sucessfully by being dramatic, nor did he want to be analytic, because
his goal in writing this novel was to satisfy readers who seemed unready
to appreciate analytic writing. Thus Conrad found himself in a dilemma
out of which he saw no way.

Nevertheless, confronted with the difficulties "The Return" caused
him, the *Rescuer* must have appeared more manageable to the author.
His renewed work on it was also stimulated by financial considerations,
because Heinemann showed interest in the manuscript: "I did send the

1ˢᵗ part of *Rescuer* to Pawling who seems *very* pleased with it," Conrad wrote to Garnett on June 2, 1897. "I *must* go on now with the *Return*—then shall jump upon the *Rescuer*" (CL I 356). Shortly after, on June 11, a dark mood took hold of him again: "I am so so . . . Thinking of *Rescuer*; writing nothing; often restraining tears; never restraining curses" (CL I 360).

In spite of it Conrad was serious in his intention to proceed with *The Rescuer* when he had finished "The Return." "Messrs. Blackwood should also be informed that for some time to come I am not likely to write any short stories," he communicated to Unwin, through whom he had begun negotiations for serial publication of his stories in *Blackwood's Edinburgh Magazine* on July 18 (CL I 356). During that summer, Conrad changed the title of his novel to *The Rescue*. When he took up direct correspondence with William Blackwood on August 28, he gave the following optimistic information: "Allow me to express the very pleasure Your enquiry as to a serial causes me . . . The story I have in hand is entitled *The Rescue: a Tale of Narrow Waters*. I began it last year but after finishing Part 1ˢᵗ laid it aside to write some short stories . . ." In the following lines he asked Mr. Blackwood's permission to send him the finished first part and expressed confidence that the novel would be completed by the end of January 1898. He ended with the following declaration: "The truth is I am very much preoccupied with the story. It'll be—apart from its subject—a deliberate attempt to get in some artistic effects of a graphic order" (CL I 376-7).

The letter that accompanied the manuscript which Conrad sent on September 6 first explained that Heinemann had offered to publish the story in book form. Then Conrad outlined his plan as to the task ahead of him:

> The situation 'per se' is not new. Consequently all the effect must be produced in the working out—in the manner of telling. This necessity from my point of view is fascinating. I am sure you will understand my feeling though you may differ with me in view. On the other hand the situation is not prosaic. It is suitable for a romance. The human interest of the tale is in the contact of Lingard the simple, masterful, imaginative adventurer with a type of civilized woman—a complex type. He is a man tenacious of purpose, enthusiastic in undertaking, faithful in friendship. He jeopardises the success of his plans first to assure her safety and then absolutely sacrifices them to what he believes the necessary condition of her happiness. He

is t[h]roughout mistrusted by the whites whom he wishes to save; he is unwillingly forced into a contest with his Malay friends. Then when the rescue, for which he had sacrificed all the interests of his life, is accomplished, he has to face his reward—an inevitable separation. This episode of his life lifts him out of himself; I want to convey in the action of the story the stress and exaltation of the man under the influence of a sentiment which he hardly understands and yet which is real enough to make him as he goes on reckless of consequences. It is only at the very last that he is perfectly enlightened when the work of rescue and destruction is ended and nothing is left to him but to try and pick up as best he may the broken thread of his life. Lingard—not the woman—is the principal personage. That's why all the first part is given up to the presentation of his personality. It illustrates the method I intend to follow. I aim at stimulating vision in the reader. If after reading the *part 1st* you don't *see* my man then I've absolutely failed and must begin again—or leave the thing alone. . . . I shall tell of some events I've seen, and also relate things I've heard. One or two men I've known—about others I've been told many interminable tales. . . . In 1848 an Englishman called Wyndham had been living for many years with the Sultan of Sulu and was the general purveyor of arms and gunpowder. . . . In the 70ies Lingard had a great if occult influence with the Rajah of Bali. He was a meddler but very disinterested and was greatly respected by the natives. As late as 1888 arms have been landed on the coast of that island—that to my personal knowledge. Thus facts can bear out my story but as I am writing fiction not secret history—facts don't matter. . . . I would take it as a very real kindness if You would tell me your opinion about the plan—and the manner of execution. . . . Of course I know I can write—in a way; I also know what I am aiming at—and it is at pure story-telling. To know that my work justifies the aim would be encouraging—to be told the reverse would be a lesson. I can only be a gainer by what You say. (CL I 381-3)

The clarity with which Conrad presented this outline contrasts with his complaint of a year earlier that the "progressive episodes of the story *will* not emerge from the chaos of [his] sensations," and thus it witnesses to the work Conrad meantime had done on the novel, even while he did not progress with its writing. It also presents the author's view of the task with which he had confronted himself and which here is called fascinating. Furthermore, it shows the trust Conrad put in Blackwood's judgment from the beginning of his acquaintance with the publisher.

The prospect to have *The Rescue* serialized in the *Maga* was extremely attractive to Conrad. Blackwood's prolonged silence due to illness disconcerted him therefore. On October 8 he wrote to Garnett, "Blackwood don't give a sign of life about the Rescue. A new serial begins in Oct. It may run six months perhaps. It would give me time to finish mine" (CL I 392). Three days later he was again in a state of depression that resembled the one which had made him abandon the novel in the previous year: "I can't get on with the *Rescue*. In all these days I haven't written a line, but there hadn't been a day when I did not wish myself dead. It's too ghastly. I positively don't know what to do" (CL I 394). Yet on October 26 he announced that he had "at last made a start with the *Rescue*" (CL I 401).

Negotiations for the serialization of *The Rescue* in *Maga* were continued at the end of October, and Conrad was elated by the erroneous assumption that Blackwood would take the novel "without reserve" (CL I 404). However, the earlier arrangement with Heinemann for the publication of the novel in book form interfered with Blackwood's interest in it. "I can only say that I regret extremely and sincerely that the *Rescue* won't appear in the Maga—since it[s] appearance as a serial there was conditional on the book going to Mr Blackwood" (CL I 406). The sentiment of regret expressed to Mr Meldrum, Blackwood's representative in London, is repeated in a letter to the editor and publisher himself. Conrad's decision to sacrifice the "good fortune to appear serially in the pages of Maga" was "simply a question of fidelity" to Heinemann, to whom Conrad felt obliged for having taken him up when he was an obscure beginner (CL I 409).

Conrad's contact with Mr. Blackwood and the hope to get his novel accepted for serial publication continued to remain serious incentives. On November 24 he wrote to the publisher that in the near future he would not have a short story to offer, because he was "wrestling with the *Rescue*" and therefore dared not think of anything else (CL I 411). In his letter to Garnett on December 5, the pessimistic note is again present: "I am trying to write the *Rescue* and all my ambition is to make it good enough for a magazine—readable in a word. I doubt whether I can. I struggle without pleasure like a man certain of defeat" (CL I 417). He is more optimistic on December 23: "I am writing the *R[escue]*! I am writing! I am harrassed with anxieties but the thing comes out! Nothing decisive has happened yet" (CL I 429).

With the arrival of his first son on January 15, 1898, Conrad's worries increased and writing did not come easier, but he continued making an effort. "I am getting on—and it is very very bad. Bad enough I sometimes think to make my fortune," he wrote to Garnett on February 2, 1898 (CL II 32). Again he tried to rid himself of his financial worries by offering his unfinished novel for serial publication. This time it was to *Saturday Review* and Cunninghame Graham was to negotiate an agreement (CL II 12,15,29).

As on the previous occasion nothing came of the planned project. In February, Conrad was able to finish Part II, and when in the same month his friend at Heinemann's, Pawling, effected the selling of the book rights to the American publisher McClure for £250, that success turned into a heavy weight around Conrad's neck. The advance payment of £100 was welcome, but for it Conrad bound himself to meet deadlines in writing a novel that still eluded him. To Pawling, he expressed the optimistic view that it could be finished in five months (CL II 42), while to C. Graham, who meantime had become the recipient of Conrad's most uninhibited expression of sentiments, the author admitted the depressing fact that there was another side of the coin: "The worst is the book is not finished yet and must be delivered end July at the latest" (CL II 44).

The consciousness of an approaching deadline, added to the strain his work on *The Rescue* caused him, resulted in a nervous disorder that was to trouble Conrad for a prolonged period of time. His letters to Garnett reflect the state of depression that afflicted the author: "I hate the thing with such great hatred that I don't want to look at it again," he wrote on March 21. Correcting himself he continued, "I shall certainly go on— that is if I can. The best about the work is that it is *sold*. They've got to take it. But the thought that such rubbish is produced at the cost of positive agony fills me with despair" (CL II 47).

The publication of *Tales of Unrest* on March 29 did not improve Conrad's mental condition:

> There's not a single word to send you. Not one! And time passes—and McClure waits . . . I seem to have lost all *sense* of style and yet I am haunted, mercilessly haunted by the *necessity* of style. And that story I can't write weaves itself into all I see, into all I speak, into all I think, into the lines of every book I try to read. . . . I tried to correct Part II[d] according to Your remarks. I did what I could—that is I knocked out a good many paragraphs. It's so much gained. As to alteration, rewriting and so on I haven't attempted it—except here and there a trifle—for

the reason I could not think out anything different to what is
written. Perhaps when I come to my senses I shall be able to do
something before the *book* comes out. As to the serial it must
go anyhow. (CL II 49-50)

Harrassed by the consciousness of his inability to meet the terms of his
contract with McClure, Conrad turned to writing "Youth," *Lord Jim*, and
essays on a variety of subjects. Among the latter, his notes on the *Sea
Stories* by Frederick Marryat and James Fenimore Cooper are of interest
especially since they appeared one day after Conrad finished "Youth"
(*Outlook*, June 4, 1898; LL I 241). They reflect the sentiments that
went into the writing of the short story and explain the ease with which
Conrad had produced it. Thereby they are an indirect comment on the
difficulties *The Rescue* was causing him.

While he was occupied with these incomparably more stimulating
subjects, Conrad's sense of responsibility and Garnett's concerned letters
reminded him of the approaching deadline. To the latter he wrote on June
7:

As to *Rescue* you are under a 'misapprehension' as Shaw would
have said. I intend to write nothing else. I am not even going to
finish Jim now. . . . The fact however remains that this *Rescue*
makes me miserable—frightens me—and I shall not abandon
it—even temporarily—I must get on with it, and it will destroy
my reputation. Sure! . . . In the matter of *R* I have lost all sense
of form and can't see *images*. But what to write I *know*. I have
the action only the hand is paralysed when it comes to giving
expression to that action. (CL II 66)

His sense of paralysis resulted in that of guilt when he thought of the
American publisher: "I am in a state of deadly, indecent funk," he wrote
to E.L. Sanderson on June 15.

I've obtained a ton of cash from a Yank under, what strikes me,
are false pretences. . . . He *thinks* the book he bought will be
finished in July while I *know* that it is a physical and intellectual
impossibility to even approach the end by that date. He sends
on regular cheques . . . I pocket them serenely, which . . . looks
uncommonly like a swindle on my part. . . . I have invited the
Yank to lunch here to-morrow. In that way I return some part
of my ill-gotten gains and may have an opportunity to break the
fatal news gently to him. (CL II 70-1)

As a result of McClure's visit to Conrad, the deadline for submitting the completed text of *The Rescue* was postponed. The relief this brought the author was of brief duration: "I thought I had months before me and am caught. . . . It is too awful. Half of the book is not written and I have only to 1ˢᵗ Novᵉʳ to finish it!" he communicated to C. Graham on August 26 (CL II 88).

Instead of decreasing, Conrad's troubles had increased. McClure had offered *The Rescue* to the *Illustrated London News* for serialization. This move should have been advantageous for Conrad since it gave him the prospect of a significantly increased income and of a wide readership. Like his contract with McClure, however, it turned into a curse: "This is sprung on me suddenly;" the author wrote to Sanderson on August 31, 1898. "I am not ready; the 'artist' is in despair; various Jews are in a rage; McClure weeps; threats of cancelling contracts are in the air—it is an inextricable mess. Dates are knocked over like ninepins; proofs torn to rags; copy rights trampled under foot. The last shred of honor is gone—also the last penny." The deadline had been postponed again: "Still I have till Novᵉʳ the 15ᵗʰ to find out whether I can dance on a tight-rope" (CL II 90).

No wonder that Conrad took steps to escape from that "inextricable mess" by trying to return to the sea. He had never totally dismissed the idea of doing so, but during the summer of 1898 his mind became increasingly preoccupied with that alternative. Encouraged by the support of C. Graham, Conrad actively searched for a command. On August 26, he had declared to that friend that he felt in honor bound to finish the novel before he could assume any other responsibility (CL II 88), but a month later he nevertheless went to Glasgow for the purpose of an interview. On September 29, he reported the result to Garnett: "Nothing decisive happened in Glasgow; my impression however is that a command will come out of it sooner or later—most likely later, when the pressing need is past and I had found my way on shore" (CL II 94). No offer was made and after this abortive attempt, Conrad did not try again to seek the solution to his problems in a return to the sea.

The trip to Glasgow did bear fruit in a different way: Conrad's spell of depression was broken. "I feel less hopeless about things and particularly about the damned thing called *the Rescue*," he concluded his report to Garnett (CL II 96). When, after two weeks, he wrote again, he commented on his mental state as follows: "I've destroyed all I did write last month but my brain feels alive and my heart is not afraid now. Permanent state?—who knows. Always hope" (CL II 103). The serialization of *The Rescue* in the *Illustrated London News* was postponed to April (to Meldrum, Oct. 12, 1898, CL II 102) and even though the thought of the unfinished novel was a lasting torment, for the time being, Conrad breathed more freely.

The improvement in the author's mental condition was accompanied by a change of environment. The Conrads rented a cottage from Ford Madox Hueffer (after WW I, Ford Madox Ford), Pent Farm, to which they transferred on October 26. "I concluded arrangement for collaboration with Hueffer," the author informed John Galsworthy two days later (CL II 112). In addition, Conrad found more opportunities for intellectual exchange with other authors since H.G. Wells, Henry James, and Stephen and Cora Crane were living in the vicinity of his new home. Despite its greater distance from London, Pent Farm offered more social life.

Occasional references to *The Rescue* in Conrad's correspondence of that period show that he still was occupied with it: "I get on dreamily with the *Rescue*," he wrote to Ford on November 12 (CL II 119). Despite the general improvement in most other matters, his mind was gloomy when concerned with that novel. "I am not well. I am eating my heart out over the rottenest book that ever was—or will be" he informed H.G. Wells on December 4 (CL II 127). But he apparently completed Part III and began Part IV before the end of the year.

While he finished "Heart of Darkness" in early February 1899, Conrad made the surprising communication that, maybe, the end of *The Rescue* was in sight. "Don't, don't ask about the Rescue. It will [be] finished about end March unless it makes an end of me before," he wrote to R.B. Cunninghame Graham on February 2 (CL II 154). Five days later, however, he gave an altogether different view of the situation to Algernon Methuen. "I am not at all sure of appearing in the Ill: London News. I've inconvenienced Mr Shorter. I know it because he said so to me in writing a few days ago. I made a suitable reply . . . And this is the last I know of the affair. However the book is promised; had been so for this year past" (CL II 157).

With the cancellation of Conrad's agreement with the *Illustrated London News*, the pressure to finish *The Rescue* was removed. McClure's patience had proven inexhaustible in the past; it would be so in the future. Besides, *Lord Jim* was occupying Conrad's mind, and on February 14, Conrad expressed his view to William Blackwood that he would do best to finish it in April (CL II 167). Thus, for the time being, *The Rescue* was laid aside. In his "Author's Note" to the novel, Conrad says the following about this step:

Several reasons contributed to this abandonment and, no doubt, the first of them was the growing sense of general difficulty in the handling of the subject. The contents and the course of the story I had clearly in my mind. But as to the way of presenting the facts, and perhaps in a certain measure as to the nature of the facts themselves, I had many doubts. I mean the telling, representative facts, helpful to carry on the idea, and, at the same time, of such a nature as not to demand an elaborate creation of the atmosphere to the detriment of the action. I did not see how I could avoid becoming wearisome in the presentation of detail and in the pursuit of clearness. I saw the action plainly enough. What I had lost for the moment was the sense of the proper formula of expression, the only formula that would suit. This, of course, weakened my confidence in the intrinsic worth and in the possible interest of the story—that is, in my invention. But I suspect that all the trouble was, in reality, the doubt of my prose, the doubt of its adequacy, of its power to master both the colours and the shades. (viii-ix)

As a task that waited for completion, *The Rescue* continued to cast its shadow over Conrad's life. On January 7, 1902, he explained the financial difficulty in which he found himself by giving the following information to Mr. Meldrum: "The last has been a disastrous year for me. I have wasted—not idled—it away, tinkering here, tinkering there—a little on *Rescue*, more on that fatal *Seraphina* with only three stories (5000 w) finished and *two* others begun lying in a drawer with no profit or pleasure to anybody" (CL II 367-8). On March 17, he explained to J.B. Pinker, who meantime had become his agent, that the work he would finish next would be *The Rescue* (CL II 394). A fire in Conrad's study on June 23, 1902, caused by the explosion of a lamp, served as an explanation why nothing came of that plan (CL II 429). He had to rewrite part of "The End of the Tether" which had been destroyed in the fire, and work on *The Rescue* was postponed again.

Still, the novel remained in the author's mind. When toward the end of 1902 Conrad's correspondence made renewed mention of the novel, he appeared to be serious about completing it. "I have been working at *Rescue* not very hard however. Still I may say that even at that rate it will be completed by March next" (CL II 456), he wrote to J.B. Pinker on November 26. On December 12, he made the acceptance of an invitation from Ernest Dawson depending on the progress which he would make with the novel: "It all depends how I get on with the story begun some six years ago and which *must* be finished in March" (CL II 462), he explained. There is no indication that Conrad actually worked on the manuscript and if he did so, how much he advanced with it. He remained diffident about the task, and at the beginning of the new year, he appealed to Hueffer hoping that his friend would achieve "the only real work of Rescue that will ever be found in [the novel's] text" (Jan. 2, 1903, CL III 4).

March arrived, and instead of having achieved the set goal, Conrad was occupied with the plan for a new novel, *Nostromo*. "Anyhow if I can finish N in 3 months I am saved for a time. And if then I can finish Rescue by Dec. next I am saved altogether. The question is—can I make the effort. Is it in me" (CL III 28). This communication, made to Ford on March 23, 1903, identifies the two poles between which Conrad's best work was produced: the inner strain of the creative effort and the outer pressure of chronic shortness of financial means.

Further mention of *The Rescue* during that period was entirely in connection with monetary considerations. As usual, the time needed for writing the next piece exeeded that calculated by Conrad. In August 1903, the author appealed to Pinker, "Try to help me out to the end of this and then we will see how we stand. . . . And then there will be nothing for it but to start at once on the Mediterranean story which is contracted for. What will become of the Rescue then devil only knows!" (CL III 55-6). *Nostromo* was finished a year later, on August 30, 1904, and in October the Conrads moved to London for three months, because Jessie's knees caused serious trouble and needed clinical care. Burdened with these additional expenses Conrad communicated to Pinker that Hueffer might be willing to help with finishing *The Rescue* if *Pall Mall Magazine* were to serialize it (Dec.21, 1904, CL III 194). No offer was made and the novel was put aside for an even longer break.

It was mentioned again in 1907 when the author explained to William Heinemann that he was not able to give his time to *The Rescue* as a main occupation, and since his spare moments were rare he saw no way to work on it at present (April 15, 1907, CL III 432). In October of the same year, he wrote to his agent: "As I told you before I intend (and think I can) squeeze in *The Rescue* into the year's work if any sort of arrangement can be made with H[einemann] and McC[lure]" (CL III 501).

The next time the novel was referred to again in Conrad's correspondence, on August 27, 1910, the author confessed that he had nearly forgotten it. It appears that J. Galsworthy, who had reminded the author of the uncompleted novel, had done so in connection with

suggestions for its publication. "Of course I will do the *Rescue*," Conrad
responded.

> I've a hazy recollection of something lightly inflated and
> verbose. But no doubt I can match it well enough out of the
> rubbish floating in my softened brain. Only I would like to
> know that Heinemann is a consenting party. . . . The book is
> H.'s absolutely,—and if I never finished it, the fragment, as it
> stands, were I to die to-morrow, would be worth £500 to him,
> unless it is an allusion of my overweening vanity. . . . My only
> objection to the *Rescue* would be that it does not advance me
> very much . . . I shall ask [Pinker] to forward me the typed copy
> of *Rescue*. It will take me a week to read and think myself into
> a proper frame of mind. (LL II 114-5)

No other mention was made of the novel, and again years passed till it
came to the surface once more.

It did so possibly as a result of the admiration André Gide expressed for
Conrad's earlier work, as Frederick Karl suggests ("Problematic Areas"
21). In any case, when Conrad took up the novel at the beginning of
1915, he hoped again to solve financial problems by getting it published
(to Pinker, Jan. 19, 1915, Berg). Correspondence with his agent Pinker
indicates that Conrad actually did some work on it while also writing *The
Shadow Line*, and on June 24, he promised to have the novel finished
before the end of the year (Feb.3, 1915; June 24, 1915; Berg). On June
8, 1916, he wrote to him as follows: "I am sending you 135 pp. of
Part IV consisting of old, (24 pp.) newly arranged, rewritten, and new
stuff" (LL II 172). His promise to finish the novel was renewed eighteen
months later with the assurance that he would "stick" to it "till the end
which [he] could see now pretty clearly" (n.d., about Dec. 1, 1916,
Berg). As so many times before, it remained a promise.

Finally, at the beginning of July 1918, Conrad braced himself for an
attack on the unfinished text that eventually was to carry him through to
the end. "With any sort of luck the Rescue will be finished this year," he
wrote to Pinker on July 5. "I am reading it over now for the 20th time at
least. I must try to catch on to the old style as much as possible. But if
I can't it will have to be done anyhow" (Berg). First, however, he still
was occupied with two essays, "First News" and "Well Done." Then, in
September, he declared to Pinker that for the time being he would not
write any short story since that would take him "too much out of the
mood for *The Rescue*" which he had "been cultivating most earnestly for

the last six weeks and [which he had] in a measure attained" by that time (Sept. 25, LL II 208).

Despite his substantially improved economic condition, Conrad does not seem to have been free from financial pressures. This is suggested by the fact that he sold the manuscript of *The Rescue* to Thomas J. Wise, although earlier it had been promised to John Quinn, a New York lawyer and collector. "You . . . are now in possession of the Ms. of a novel that certainly will not be published till 1920" he wrote to Mr. Wise on October 2.

> This Ms. also holds a special position in so far that it is the only one which has a history extending over twenty years. Begun in 1896 as my third planned novel, it was laid aside finally at the end of '99, so that a whole pile of pages belongs wholly to the Nineteenth Century. The preservation of those pages I owe certainly to my wife, who insisted on keeping them in one of her drawers long after I lost all interest in the Ms. as Ms., for several typed copies have been taken of it, each introducing changes and alterations till this last (I believe the 4th) typed copy on which I am working now, and I intend to finish the tale by dictating. Thus you will understand that there will be no further pen and ink pages. The first complete state of the novel will be a typed copy bearing pen and ink corrections and alterations." (LL II 209)

One of the copies to which Conrad referred in that letter obviously was in the possession of F.N. Doubleday, because writing to L.F. Hartman on July 26, 1918, Doubleday states: "I am sending you a confidential manuscript of the incomplete story of 'The Rescue,' by Mr. Conrad. In my opinion, it is one of the best things he has done; but, as you see, it is not yet completed . . . " (Berg).

Seven days after Conrad had written to T.J. Wise, he explained to his friend Richard Curle that unfavorable circumstances had made him lay aside *The Rescue* for some time, but that now "it shall be taken up with vigour" and that it was "expected to achieve a success by January next at the latest" (Oct. 9, 1918, *Conrad to a Friend* 51). By the end of November, Conrad finished Part IV (to Pinker, Nov. 21, 1918, Berg) and on December 21, he informed F.N. Doubleday: "*The Rescue* is approaching completion and I believe that the last words will be written before the end of January. The serialization of that story will be another problem in which, if opportunity offers, I feel I can count upon your assistance" (LL II 215).

When at the end of 1918 it came to actual negotiations for serialization in *Cosmopolitan Magazine*, Conrad was more realistic as to the time still needed for the novel's completion. His letter to Pinker, who was to negotiate the publication, is of much interest since it bears witness to the change which the author's opinion on the events and issues that matter in the novel had undergone with the passage of time:

> As to any sort of synopsis of events, . . . I am afraid it would be of no help because the interest of that romance is all in the shades of the psychology of the people engaged, as is obvious from the four parts already completed. It is sustained by the presentation alone. You may however assure the representative of the *Cosmopolitan Magazine* that the story will end as romantically as it began, and that no one of any particular consequence will have to die. Hassim and Immada will be sacrificed, as in any case they were bound to be, but their fate is not the subject of the tale. All those yacht people will go on their way, leaving Lingard alone with the wreck of the greatest adventure of his life. For indeed what else could have happened? Any tragedy there is in this *dénouement* will be all in the man's feelings; and whatever value there may be in that, must depend on the success of the romantic presentation. . . . There are many kinds of romance and this one is not fit for juvenile readers, not because it raises any sort of problem but on account of the depth and complexity of the feelings involved in the action, which in itself does not aim at any great originality and can be pretty well forseen from the beginning. (LL II 212)

Twenty-one years earlier Conrad had declared that the novel was intended to become a "glorified book for boys." Compared with that proposition, the last sentence of the above quotation exposes the immense gap between what the author had intended to do and what his artistic intuition ultimately had led him to. It is an eloquent comment on his prolonged inability to get ahead with the novel.

Although not yet completed at the end of January 1919, the novel began to appear in print. *Land and Water* started its serialization on January 30 (Najder 439) and on the same day, the author assured Pinker of his renewed concentration on finishing the novel. "The production of further copy shall begin on Thursday morning next." Referring to the publication of *The Rescue* and *The Arrow of Gold*, he continued, "I hope one of those two books will make a hit—I mean a money hit. I fancy it is *The Rescue*, which is picturesque and at the same time more conventional, that will prove the best spec. of the two" (LL II 219).

The author's expectation proved to be realistic. On April 17 he could thank Doubleday for having successfully negotiated the serialization of the novel in America, and then he assured him that it had received a warm welcome among English readers: "I am glad to say that the proprietors of *Land and Water* profess themselves very pleased by the reception given to the serial here, and by its good effect on the circulation of the paper" (LL II 221).

These words might be taken as an example of the author's tendency to make his works appear in a better light when corresponding with his publishers than in letters to friends. But there is evidence that during that stage of the novel's development Conrad looked on it with more satisfaction than ever before. When he learned that members of the Athenaeum Club considered his nomination for the Order of Merit, Conrad expressed strong doubts whether he would qualify for that honor. But he also indicated that he was not disinclined to accept the Nobel Prize if it were offered to him. The book that might earn him that distinction, he calculated, could be *The Rescue*. "I think sincerely," he wrote to Pinker on February 15, "that 'Rescue' has a particular quality. Novels of adventure will, I suppose, be always written; but it may well be that 'Rescue' in its concentrated colouring and tone will remain the swan song of Romance as a form of literary art" (Berg).

Meanwhile the novel was still growing. On February 22, Conrad calculated that he would reach the end by adding fifty more pages (to Doubleday, Princeton), but on March 12, he was still ninety pages from the end (to Pinker, March 11 or 12, 1919, Berg). His concentration on writing was interrupted by the necessity to leave Capel House. On March 25 the Conrads moved to Spring Grove, and from there Conrad informed Pinker on April 11 that he had begun the "penultimate chapt. of *Rescue*. The last will be very short. I am by no means sick of the *R*. but oh! what a relief it will be!" (Berg). In fact, Conrad was to add not one but three more chapters before, on May 25, 1919, he could put the final period to the dictated typescript (Najder 594n239; to Pinker, May 29, 1919, Berg).

The completion of *The Rescue* brought Conrad the relief after which he had been yearning for over twenty years. The serialization of the novel in *Land and Water*, which ran through July 1919, and the American one in *Romance* from November 1919 through May 1920 were unquestioned successes. In December 1919 and January 1920, Conrad revised the magazine version for book publication. When on May 21,

1920, Doubleday published the novel in book form and Dent in August of the same year, the reviewers responded with enthusiastic admiration. "Of the style it would now be superfluous to speak," an anonymous reviewer wrote in *Punch*. "It has been given to Mr. Conrad, working in what is originally a foreign medium, to use it with a dignity unsurpassed by any of our native craftsmen" (CH 336). "His book is an amazing study of atmosphere, spiritual and physical," another reviewer, who then skillfully proceeded by making the novel's faults appear as its advantages, wrote in *Nation* (CH 340).

The satisfaction Conrad derived from the novel was modest. He was fully conscious of its shortcomings, and the few voices that were frank enough to point them out touched his sensitivity more keenly precisely because of the general adulation which the novel received. Among them was the unsigned review of Virginia Woolf in *The Times Literary Supplement*:

> But if the statement of the theme is extremely fine, we have to admit that the working out of the theme is puzzling; we cannot deny that we are left with a feeling of disappointment. . . . Is there anything in man or woman, scene or setting, unworthy or jarring upon our senses? If anything, the setting is too flawless in its perfection and the characters too fixed in their nobility. Mr. Conrad has never striven harder to heap up beauty of scene and romance of circumstance until the slightest movement tells like that of an actor upon the stage. . . . The elements of tragedy are present in abundance. If they fail to strike one unmistakable impression upon us, it is, we think, because Mr. Conrad has attempted a romantic theme and in the middle his belief in romance has failed him. (CH 333-5)

Did Conrad's belief in romance fail him? He did not think so; the letter to Pinker in which he expressed his confidence as to the value of *The Rescue* calling it a "swan song of Romance" and another one written on the same day to Mr Cecil Roberts in which he said "I have thrown into that tale . . . all that I am, all that I have, in the way of romantic vision, expression, and feeling" (Feb. 15, 1919) suggest the opposite. If he nevertheless fails to achieve the desired effect the reasons, although they are varied, are more likely to be found in Conrad's failure to write the novel from the depth of his "inwardness" which, according to his words to Noble, was essential for success.

II ROMANTIC CHIVALRY VERSUS POLITICAL ROMANCE

The short preface-like opening of *The Rescue* is an effective key to the novel. At a first approach, it suggests to the reader the qualities of a panegyric with a simple explanation for Conrad's repeated returns to the Malay Archipelago in his early fiction. Catch phrases such as "mystery and romance of the past," "adventurous undertakings," "love of liberty" suggest nostalgia and encourage the approach that the readers of Conrad's early fiction mostly have taken and which furthermore has resulted in a sense of frustration on their part as well as on that of the author.

Examined for their true value within the context, these phrases reveal themselves as greatly misleading. For what is presented as a veil of mystery and romance hides the gruesome reality of the historical past of the Archipelago, one of fights, conquests, and the "unavoidable defeat" of the Malays by four European nations. Pitted against the nostalgic reference to the colonial enterprise of known and unknown adventurers is the unmistakable admiration paid to the Malays for their resilience in preserving their characteristic qualities. The vices and virtues of the conquerors are countered by the "lawful and unlawful instincts" of the conquered. A common bond exists between the disinterested adventurer and obscure lawbreakers, and what appeared to be an enthusiastic tribute to the colonial past thus becomes a questioning of that which seemed to be eulogized. As the brief preface serves as an exposition to the themes of this novel, the reader is sensitized to inherent ironies and warned to allow for the author's shifting sympathies in developing them.

The difficult, prolonged process of creating *The Rescue* has left its marks on the finished novel. A comparison of the book with "The Rescuer" manuscript is rewarding inasmuch as it offers clues to some of the inconsistencies in plot and character development obvious in the former. It especially helps to identify the passions and ambitions of Lingard.

In "The Rescuer" they are of a prevailingly political nature. Despite Lingard's claim not to meddle with the interests of the Dutch, his planned war on Wajo is a conscious revolt against the consolidation of European powers in the East. Therefore it is to take place while the English squadron is away preparing for war on China, the French are "raising the devil in Cambodja, and the Dutchmen are asleep" (34). Being a trader who outdoes even the "sharpest Chinaman" (14), Lingard's interests are identical with those of Hassim, the "ideal trader of Wajo," whose engagements are as much of a diplomatic as of an economic nature (121). "Trading thus understood was the occupation of ambitious men," the narrator explains in "The Rescuer" after Hassim has been introduced,

> they played an occult but important part in all those national risings, religious disturbances and in the organized piratical movements on a large scale which during the first half of the present century affected the fate of more than one native dynasty and, for a few years at least, seriously endangered the Dutch rule in the East. (121-2)

On the surface, Lingard is motivated by sentimental pity for Immada and by the desire to give to justice, gratitude, and friendship what is their due. But the impulse on which he acts shows the cause of the Wajo prince as an opportunity to make history by making war. In "The Rescuer" Lingard sees in the circumstances "mysterious possibilities," "a suggestion of power to be picked up by a strong hand." These ambitions take hold of Lingard's whole existence. They "possessed themselves of his thoughts, of his activity, of his hopes—in an inevitable and obscure way even of his affections" (187).

The manuscript suggests that Lingard's infatuation with Edith Travers makes him lose sight of that project only for a short time. This is obvious from the lengthy discourse on the subject of his political ambitions in the last chapters, which are not included in the book. Still on their nightly boat trip to the *Emma*, Lingard acquaints Edith Travers with the history of Wajo, explaining to her that fifty years earlier the grandfather of his Malay friends headed a confederacy of four states, which was broken up by the Dutch when the English ceded the islands to them (566). Lingard is determined to restore the confederacy; to

> make them take their stand in the world . . . Against anybody,
> against anything; face to the Dutch and back to the sea . . . The
> four states welded together, by his hand; the land awakened,
> living, breathing; growing strong enough not to be meddled
> with. His work! His! And if he once went in he would not
> come out—never. (570)

The readiness for total surrender which is expressed here renders his
form of surrender in *The Rescue* more ironic.

By the omission from the book of many passages that in "The Rescuer"
clearly show Lingard's project as an intended subversion of the intersts of
European colonial authorities and his motivation as rooted in ambitions
for power, the emphasis and attention of the narrative shift to Lingard's
conflict of divided loyalties. Occasional traces of the author's original
intentions pass unnoticed or obscure rather than illumine the context.
Indications of hostilities between the English and the Dutch tend to be
seen against the general historical background more than that of Lingard's
unlawful preoccupations, and with the diminished importance of the
political romance the soft romance with the English society lady gains
in scope.

The change in the Lingard-Hassim relationship that results from this
is the increased importance of the aspect of friendship which gradually
serves as an indicator of King Tom's downward development. Their
friendship becomes the backdrop and frame to the story of the white
man in *The Rescue*. After their first encounter on the shores of New
Guinea, which establishes it, Hassim is present in Lingard's life at all its
pivotal points. Their meeting in Wajo results in his pledge to become
a political savior; on the *Hermit* Hassim witnesses the beginning of
Lingard's insecurity as Mr Travers challenges his credibility and with
it the identity he has created for himself in the East; in Lingard's cabin
Hassim is present as the crucial choice is made to go after the kidnapped
Europeans, which decides the future of them all; and on the *Emma*
Hassim is the ultimate reminder of Lingard's earlier pledge of constancy
in friendship. From their first handshake to that for which Hassim longs
in the face of death, this relationship is a continuous testing ground of the
viability of friendship between Europeans and Malays. Within the context
of European colonial history, it becomes a document that investigates its
justifiability.

The ironic incongruities of the short preface reappear in the
circumstances under which this friendship is established. With the
first handshake over the prostrate body of the Malay who died for

Lingard's recklessness, the author gives away his outlook on the resulting relationship. He speaks of friendship as fate's "most ominous" gift (73) and thereby proffers an early answer to the question suggested above. In addition to the loss of a life, the Malays pay for this relationship with the forfeiture of promising opportunities for trade. Lingard, in turn, acknowledges his indebtedness with three barrels of gunpowder. Hassim, the younger man, displays restraint and deliberation—qualities that might be expected of the older partner. But on account of the superior economic and political strength of England, with which Hassim identifies him, Lingard assumes the role of a protector. He accepts the credit which the Malay gives him on the basis of his race and nationality. Yet he also admits that the identity by which he recognizes himself, that of "King Tom," has been acquired in the eastern seas and is bound up with the opportunities which that part of the world grants him. To emphasize this he juxtaposes the yacht people to his Malay friends, Hassim and Immada, as he says to Mrs Travers, "What are you to me against these two?" (158); and later, "You're no more mine than I am yours" (165).

With the decision to make Hassim's cause his own, Lingard's vaccillating self-identification becomes problematic and the irony of it poignant. To procure the necessary means and allies, he takes advantage of the opportunities and privileges he enjoys as a European, and by doing so he prepares to challenge and undermine what he relies on. He becomes lawless in order to serve justice; he enlists the help of a pacifist to prepare for war; and he means to restore property to its lawful owner by employing pirates.

Lingard's lack of sound judgment is obvious, but his confused and complicated motivations escape not only his own recognition; in *The Rescue* they are not easily identified even by the reader. As in "The Rescuer," his conscious intentions are to serve justice. Evidence as to his personal aims is scarce, although not altogether absent. Lingard admits, for instance, that his passionate nature finds satisfaction in fighting as he concludes the story of the Frenchman and the girl of Bali by saying, "That was the first time in my life I nearly went to war on my own account" (21). Likewise, he looks on his engagement for Hassim's cause as a "chance" (157). Together with his declaration "I am a white man inside and out" (39), these examples show the gap between the interests Lingard and Hassim bring to the undertaking to regain power in Wajo. For Lingard it is an opportunity to strengthen his position as a white man among the Malays, but the social aspect which Hassim points out to him with the assurance that in Wajo Lingard will be honored like the prince's father is of little value to him because of his white-man consciousness.

The inner dichotomy which manifests itself in Lingard's simultaneous assertion and rejection of his identity as a European incapacitates him to pursue his political project with consistency. It is at the root of the irony that colors most of his relationships, and it causes the dilemma that carries the plot forward. For with the arrival of representatives of fashionable English society on the Shore of Refuge, Lingard is forced to declare his choice. He does so with the promise to Edith Travers "Not a hair of your head shall be touched as long as I live!" (164). Since he can explain his perplexity only by the practical problem of the presence of the yacht in a strategically important point, those words witness to his hopeless state of confusion, and the reader is warned to allow for more complex reasons underlying them.

In "The Rescuer" Conrad prepared for the disconcerting effect which the arrival of the Europeans has on Lingard by hinting that despite his seemingly rough nature Lingard was over- sensitive and basically insecure. When his friends keep distant in consequence of the secrecy with which he surrounds himself as he prepares for war on Wajo, he feels isolated and judged by them. He becomes conscious of having a dark side to his life. "It hurt him. . . . Nobody knew what he was doing but all the same everybody seemed to disapprove of it" (171). Conrad omitted this passage from the book, but he retained the idea of Lingard's sensitivity to the opinion of others as his reaction to Mr Travers' offensive attitude soon demonstrates.

In *The Rescue* Lingard's insecurity is caused by his low social origin. Because he is sensitive to racial and social distinctions, his self-assurance is seriously shaken by the presence of Travers and his party in the shallows of the Shore of Refuge. Lingard denies the significance of social status when he challenges that of Mr Travers, a British financier and politician, with the flat question, "who is he?" (154). But the keenness with which his pride registers that man's refusal to shake hands with him, the son of a fisherman and the ex-Brixham trawler-boy, betrays the importance which Lingard attaches to that denial of their social equality. Pride, in addition to moral sense and racial consciousness, impels him therefore to assume the role of a protector to the white people, even before his infatuation for Mrs Travers obliges him to do so. "You must understand that you have nothing to give," he tells Edith when she proposes to avert danger from all of them by offering ransom money. In face of Daman's determination to loot the yacht, of which Lingard is fully aware, his rejection of any way out of their precarious situation other than by his own mediation testifies to Lingard's need to prove himself as equal to them in importance.

His insecurity accounts for the weight Lingard attaches to being understood correctly, and it explains the romantic vulnerability that results from thinking Edith Travers capable of it. It is on account of her words "I believe you meant to be friendly to us" (143) that he returns to the yacht after nightfall and that he pledges to keep her from harm. In its different tenses and combinations 'understand' is a much used word in the novel, and in nearly two thirds of all cases it refers in some way to Lingard and his activities; it abounds especially in his conversations with Edith Travers.

Because Lingard feels insecure he recognizes in Mr Travers a threat to his status as "King Tom." Travers travels to study the Dutch colonial system in order to "expose" it; in "The Rescuer" he studies "the impact of western progress upon the races of the East" (225). Lingard clearly understands that Travers is an advocate of European policies that aim at the centralization of power and capitalistic exploitation. His presence is a challenge to Lingard's patriarchal position among the Malays and to the identity he has created for himself. In addition to the need to preserve his superior white-man image among the indigenous population by the rescue of the kidnapped Europeans, Lingard also recognizes that he needs to prove his mode of existence as necessary in order to justify and redeem it in the eyes of the Europeans.

The polarity of Lingard and Travers expresses itself pointedly in the opinion each holds of what is most important to the other—his work. To Lingard Travers' scientific involvement in imperialistic concerns is play; but to the latter Lingard's occupation among the local population is criminal and therefore a disgrace to civilization. Despite their similaritiy in age, they represent two successive eras in the development of European imperialism, and Lingard's insistence that the dilemma of the yacht people cannot be solved by means provided by capitalism rather than those his prestigious position can secure acquires additional significance.

Lingard's relation to Edith Travers is therefore not so much a "reflex toward submission" to the socially superior, as John A. McClure suggests (119), as it is a means toward self-elevation and self-affirmation. When he lets go of his life project, Lingard appears to become subject to the lady's expectations. But as he assures himself of her trust, dependence, and seeming understanding, as he finds in her a recipient of his confidences and a companion on his boat trips, he experiences himself rewarded with a sense of equality with her and the class she represents. If the erotic element in their relation explains much of the satisfaction he derives from a handshake with her, it is to the same degree the result of his need to redeem his social self-image. The hours spent at her feet in total oblivion of reality are climactic also when looked at from this angle.

Edith Travers registers correctly this dimension of her relation to Lingard: "she was aware of something that resembled gratitude and provoked a sort of emotional return as between equals who had secretly recognized each other's value" (283). Despite his general obtuseness, even Mr Travers is well aware of the social significance Lingard attaches to that relationship. He proves this as he upraids his wife saying, "I can't credit you with the possession of feelings appropriate to your origin, social position, and the ideas of the class to which you belong" (267). His social prejudice does not allow for an elevation of the buccaneer; therefore his wife's contact with that man is by necessity a lowering of her social status.

Lingard, however, sees himself confirmed in his worth by the fact that Edith Travers entrusts her safety to his care, and after her transfer to his brig, his self-identification is with the white people of the yacht. His lack of introspection accounts for the truthfulness with which his verbal utterances reflect his shifting loyalties. He begins to speak of the Europeans as "my people" and admits that Hassim's cause is no longer his own as he says, "Are they waiting for what will never come now?" (227).

Ironically, instead of giving him more self-assurance and confidence, these developments isolate Lingard and leave him emotionally and politically adrift. He remains ignorant of the fact that to Edith Travers the most obvious truth about his life is his lawlessness. But he is keenly aware of his loss of credibility in consequence of his divided allegiances, and eventually he arrives at the recognition of the traitorous potential inherent in them. When he abandons the brig, he knows that with it he not only abandons Hassim's interests but also the hope to defuse the highly explosive state of affairs among the heterogeneous groups of Malays whom he has made his allies. Thus it is not Mr Travers and what he represents that threatens Lingard's status so much as his own vaccillating loyalty, and with the explosion of the *Emma* the existence he has built for himself as a colonial authority is shattered in consequence of what he himself is.

If he remains in the dark as to the deepest causes of his inner confusion, and if the reader is inclined to ascribe it mainly to sexual attraction, the author offers illumination and a corrective in the person of Joergenson. Alone by virtue of his involvement in Lingard's political scheme, Joergenson functions as a witness to the loyalties and obligations Lingard has chosen earlier, and thereby his role as an advocate of

Hassim's cause is established. Due to the relativity of human liabilities, however, this function would be of limited value were it not forcefully supported by the witness of his own career.

When Joergenson first attaches himself to Lingard, he is called a "haunting spirit from the past eager to step back into the life of men" (98). In so far as his past and present illustrate the possibilities inherent in Lingard's divided state of mind, Joergenson serves as its objective correlative. Lingard recognizes himself in the one when— though reluctantly—he admits to Edith Travers that Joergenson is "a man like myself" (157). However, his lack of reflection hides from him the truth that Joergenson's total detachment from the privileges and opportunities his status as a white man has offered him earlier is not merely the result of ill luck, but of a conscious choice based on principles that Lingard also claims to uphold: honor and fidelity. Joergenson says of himself that he speaks all the dialects of the Malay islands in addition to English and Dutch, the languages of the colonial powers; his mother tongue he has forgotten and with it the claims that are attached to his western origin. They have died with his barque and his position as its captain. Seen from the aspect of his colonial involvement, his "going native" in acknowledgement of the ties he has formed with the local people is a proof of consistency and moral strength rather than of deterioration. But having become one with the indigenous people, Joergenson is no longer of any consequence. When Belarab visits him, he does so for what the white man has been, not for what he is.

By the presence of Joergenson as his shadow when Lingard prepares to interfere with the politics of Wajo, the latter is exhorted to acknowledge the only alternative that justifies meddling with the concerns of the natives, which is, disinterested pursuance of their benefits. However, the reason Lingard gives for the state of the older man's affairs—"More sense, perhaps, but less luck" (157)—in addition to his inability to account for his own motivations explains why the lesson of Joergenson is lost on him.

Likewise is that suggested by the polarity of Edith Travers and Immada. The thematic importance of the confrontation of these two women is obvious. To make the indigenous girl more of a qualified rival to the English society lady, Conrad has chosen a princess who is not only fully conscious of her status but also determined to claim what is her due. In the omitted late portions of "The Rescuer" light is thrown on the contrast between brother and sister which shows Hassim as slower and gentler than the girl by mention of their mother who ruled Wajo when the confederate states were separated by the Dutch. "A great woman but an unlucky one in many ways" (566), Lingard comments on that period of Wajo history and the woman who has shaped it. The implication is that in Immada's personality traces of a matriarchal society are inherent.

It is in keeping with Lingard's attitude towards women in the previous novels that, despite his recognition of the potential Immada has for leadership, his sentiment for her is only pity. To him the project to regain Wajo is a concern of men and a matter of justice towards Hassim. Therefore the truths that become apparent in the meeting of the two women escape him. Only his emotions respond to their appeal, and since he neither understands these nor knows how to control them, the contest between the two women for his loyalty is decided when it has hardly begun.

From the very start it is a conscious and determined contest. The Malay girl is present as the English woman enters Lingard's life. In their differences—one dark, gentle, promising, the other fair, firm, mature— the two worlds to which they belong are contrasted. D'Alcacer likens this difference to the "superiority of the flower over the leaf, of the phrase that contains a thought over the cry that can only express an emotion" (140). Each recognizes in the other the rival. For, despite the protective superiority which Edith Travers displays towards Immada, she correctly estimates the advantages that are inherent in the freedom from the limiting civilization to which she herself belongs.

It is significant that in the first as well as in all subsequent encounters of the two women with Lingard, narrative references to sight and sound effects abound. Edith Travers appeals mainly to Lingard's sense of vision, Immada to that of hearing. Like the continent from which she comes, the former suggests supple splendor in the same way as the girl's "shy resolution" and passionate entreaties are expressive of the undefined possibilities of the world that has formed her. Her repeated attempts to make that world assert itself as she exhorts Lingard to avert his gaze from the white woman remain ineffective, because they are not reciprocated by the mental process necessary to affect conscious decisions.

Lingard's unreflective response to the presence of the Europeans decides the issue before he is aware of his being subject to a change. His roots and moral ties, made visible to him by the yacht and its occupants, are more tangible than the future that attaches to the girl of whom he says that he loves her like a daughter. While he claims to pursue the interests of his Malay friends, he begins to forget them. Because Lingard is tainted by his self-consciousness as a European, he is unable to rescue the values which Immada represents. The interpretation he gives to the strategy of Daman in kidnapping the two white men is therefore highly ironic: "it was perhaps a great folly to trust any white man, no matter how much he seemed estranged from his own people" (296). With these words in which his subconscious expresses itself, Lingard inadvertently admits the truth about himself and his aspirations in friendship with the indigenous people.

The degree to which Edith Travers' visual appeal outweighs that of Immada's words finds expression in the "image" of the white woman that Lingard takes with him back to the brig. In addition to his need for security that finds support in the notion that Edith Travers understands him, his infatuation originates in his special sensitivity to visual impressions. The author's intention to please his readers explains much of the scope Conrad allows for romantic love in this novel. But it has been seen that when he planned *An Outcast* Conrad indirectly admitted his ineptness at handling this theme and his difficulty with it is reflected in the confusion chivalry and sexual attraction create in Lingard and for the reader. The author's complaint to Garnett that Lingard, the seaman, eluded him (CL I 289), corresponds with the observation of Edith Travers that she "cannot . . . imagine [Lingard] at all" (149), by which she means to say that she does not recognize the Englishman in Lingard.

To cope with the problem of Lingard as a lover, Conrad obviously resorted to portraying in him qualities of the Polish *szlachta* from which the author himself derived. In it chivalric values were dominant, as Zdzislaw Najder states (3), and these were the inheritance of the Polish romantic tradition in which questions of moral responsibility are approached from the social aspect of duties and responsibilities rather than from that of conscience and self-perfection. Thus the Lingard of the love story is different from Lingard, the master of his craft who is introduced early in the novel as loving his vessel with "a man's love." It is an exacting love that tries the faithfulness of his brig *Lightning* "to the very utmost limit of endurance" (54), and the steadfastness with which the ship responds to Lingard's demands on her is to him an inspiration and source of emotional satisfaction. The passage serves as a point of reference to measure the change from the early Lingard to the man who says to Edith late in the novel that she has "taken all hardness" out of him (339).

As a matter of fact, in the author's conception of the protagonist, this change has been prepared for from the beginning. In "The Rescuer" the above passage is preceded by the earlier, surprising observation that the intense experiences of interacting with his craft brought about a listlessness in Lingard that became noticeable in his appearance as a weakening. "It was one of his peculiarities," the narrator explains, "that whenever he had to call upon his unerring knowledge of his craft upon his skill and readiness in matters of his calling that big body of his lost its alertness, seemed to sink a little as if some inward prop had been suddenly withdrawn" (95). Conrad did not include this passage in the book and thereby he allowed for a greater contrast between the man as captain of his brig and as a romantic lover. However, the passage shows the consistency with which the author developed the Lingard character according to the originally conceived plan which allowed for Lingard's "temporary foolishness," and the emasculation of the protagonist in the later part of the novel is accordingly not a consequence of Conrad's declining powers as a novelist but of the prolonged presence of Edith Travers in the life of Lingard.

With the absence of the above passage from the book, Lingard's act of relinguishing the brig becomes more one of infidelity, self-exposure, and romantic adventure. For, since the inanimate vessel is essential for the man's experience of himself as an animate being, of his mental and emotional capacities, above all, of his will power, he is adrift in every way when he separates from it. To the degree that he loses touch with his brig, he loses hold on reality and on his capacity for exercising his will.

In the drama of love, this process begins with Lingard's farewell to the ship when in the darkness of night he goes to escort Edith Travers from the *Hermit* to his brig. His misinterpretation of the way she responds to him causes Lingard moments of bliss, but leaves him mostly disturbed and unhappy. His inability to understand her power over him and—resulting from this—his helplessness combine with the insecurity that obliges him to prove himself and result in the mixture of desire and honor that characterizes his chivalry.

The disastrous consequences of Lingard's meeting with Edith are early foreshadowed in the conversation of the officers about the Balinese flower girl and Helen of Troy. By this combination of an example from ancient times with one contemporary to the narrator, the universality of the experience is emphasized and that of Lingard prepared for. Considered together, the two accounts arouse the reader's awareness of the social aspect of an individual's experience as an early warning against the consequences of Lingard's infatuation.

It is fitting that Lingard separate from Edith Travers at the grave of Jaffir, and since he does, the disaster of his folly is not the final message of the novel. When Conrad expressed his belief that *The Rescue* might earn him the Nobel Prize, he gave to understand that this "Romance of the Shallows" did not end in the death of Lingard's Malay friends, but in the message that the grave contains. It is a message of trust and goodwill where hatred and cynicism might have been expected. It witnesses to a spiritual strength that is not subject to destruction by dynamite nor confinable to a grave.

There is therefore a note of hopefulness in the ending of this novel which echoes the praise of the lasting endurance of what is genuinely Malay, which is expressed in the brief preface of the novel. Within the context of a study of Conrad's views on European imperialism, it is significant that the white man is the recipient of this hope. Lingard who has been accustomed to the role of a giver has become the receiver of a generosity that challenges him to face the reality of his life again. At the grave of Jaffir he picks up the fragments of his former existence in order to make a new start. The belief expressed in this conclusion of the "Romance of the Shallows" obviously is that Europe may trust in its future because of the forgiveness of those it has tried to dominate. It is the undiminished strength of a people not weakened by the insincerities of European civilization that can offer that forgiveness.

III THE MANNER OF TELLING

When in the fall of 1897 Conrad wrote to William Blackwood, the publisher whom he hoped to interest in *The Rescue*, he summed up the difficulty which the writing of this novel caused him in the following statement: "The situation 'per se' is not new. Consequently all the effect must be produced in the working out—in the manner of telling" (CL I 381). "It's most damnably hard," he admitted to Garnett (CL I 396). In 1918, as Conrad braced himself to complete the novel, he explained to his agent Pinker, "I must try to catch on to the old style as much as possible. But if I can't it will have to be done anyhow" (July 5, Berg). Instead of trying to force himself into the style of his early years, however, Conrad resorted to the solution of fitting the text of twenty years earlier to the style he meanwhile had developed. Extensive changes and cuttings in the original text were to adjust it to the newly added one.

The result is an obvious imbalance of two unequal halves. "The Rescuer" manuscript shows that before putting it away in the early months of 1899, Conrad had finished the first three parts of the novel and much of the fourth one. The text he retained from this constitutes slightly more than one half of the book which he completed in 1918 and the first months of 1919 by adding parts five and six. With the decisive scene in Lingard's stateroom on his brig *Lightning*, the climax of the book is reached in the later half of part four, so that one third of the total of six parts has to balance the preceding two thirds. By the changes Conrad made in the first half through cutting the text in many places it became more tightly structured. In comparison, the last two parts give an impression of rambling loseness.

The element of time, which throughout the novel is of eminent importance, accounts for much of that unevenness. Conrad worked under the pressure of his advanced age; had he distanced himself from the last two parts in time as he had from parts one through four he probably would have shortened them likewise. But the less tangible and more important reason is that the passage of time had brought with it a change in the role of the protagonist.

Concluding from the treatment of the theme of imperialism in "The Rescuer" with its frequent references to hostilities between the English and the Dutch, and especially from the presentation of Lingard as being in the grip of political ambitions, the turning point in the protagonist's story came in part three, "The Capture." With the presence of the English yacht in the Shallows, both Lingard's political project and his peace of heart are brought to the testing point, and the question to be decided in the rest of the novel was to be that of conflicting interests rather than of loyalties.

The modifications which Conrad made in the early finished parts led to a shift of emphasis. Since Lingard's political scheme is no longer clearly recognizable in its full weight of being a project in direct defiance of the rights of the Dutch, potentially explosive in its consequences, the values that are seen at stake at the turning point of the book are loyalty and friendship versus romantic chivalry.

The changes which Conrad also made in his presentation of the protagonist likewise contributed to this shift of climax. With the absence from the book of those passages that in "The Rescuer" show Lingard as overly sensitive and insecure, he appears as a stronger man than originally conceived. He becomes misleading, for under the surface of his simplicity and strength there is his complexity which increasingly asserts itself with its desires and needs and the resulting motivations and responses. When he ends his state of being torn between the alternatives among which he has to choose with the decision to save the two white men in order to save himself, he escapes from reality into an illusion. It is significant that, as in the case of Willems who surrenders to his passion for an indigenous woman, Conrad employs the image of a drowning swimmer in narrating this step of Captain Lingard. Thus the turning point becomes Lingard's act of relinquishing the brig of which he has said that it gives substance to his life. This starts the chain of events that upon his awakening leave him with the ruins of the existence he has built for himself among the Malays.

Conrad's "manner of telling" Lingard's story resembles that of the first two novels in his frequent reliance on the effects achieved by time shifts. Part one, "The Man and the Brig," serves as an introduction to the larger setting of the novel and its themes, but especially to its protagonist. "If after reading the *part 1ˢᵗ* you don't *see* my man then I've absolutely failed and must begin again—or leave the thing alone" (CL I 382), with these words Conrad emphasised the importance of the Lingard character. Through the creation of an atmosphere that suggests hidden dangers, the omniscient narrator transmits an awareness of the potentially dangerous form of existence of the protagonist, and with the arrival of the boat from the yacht complication begins to build up. The storm through which the brig passes in approaching the stranded vessel is the objective correlative to the sentiments that take hold of the protagonist as he realizes the implications of Carter's news. But the mastery he displays in handling the ship as the storm hits serves as a foiling contrast to the later inefficiency in dealing with the presence of the yacht in the Shallows.

Part two, "The Shore of Refuge," introduces the reader to the immediate scene of the events. The extensive reflections on the historical past of the Shallows, which in the manuscript open this part, are excluded from the book; the leading sentiments are condensed into the panegyric-like opening to the novel. Enough of the original atmosphere is preserved in the introduction to this part, however, to foreshadow the final results of the impending events.

With the introduction of Hassim and Immada, a time shift back to the beginning of the friendship with the white trader is prepared for, and in the following chapter a full-length account of it is given. The retrospective narrative continues in the subsequent chapters showing Lingard briefly in the company of his peers as an opportunity for providing a professional evaluation of the protagonist as a trader, Lingard's approach to Wajo, which parallels chapter three of part one in its sequence of a calm followed by a storm with their symbolic implications, the rescue of the besieged party of the ousted prince, Lingard's decision to restore Hassim to his political rights, the beginning of Joergenson's involvement in the project and Lingard's alliance with the pacifist Belarab. To strengthen reader awareness as to the bearing these events have on the things that happen in the simple past, the narrator repeatedly takes a brief step forward to it at the beginning of a new chapter.

Part three, "The Capture," which originally was to bring the climax, begins in the midst of Lingard's conversation with Mr Travers on the stranded yacht *Hermit*. This is briefly interrupted to give the reader a glimpse into the protagonist's mental and emotional disposition and a superficial introduction to Travers' companions. With the casual observation of d'Alcacer that "There is liking at first sight as well as love at first sight" (130), the element of romantic love is announced in chapter three, and the interest of Edith Travers in the protagonist is aroused and further stimulated in the following chapter by the surmise that Lingard loves the Malay princess Immada.

In this way the stage is set for Lingard's return after nightfall, as that for the kidnapping of Travers and d'Alcacer is prepared for by the foreboding the latter has in chapter five. Lingard's nightly visit to the yacht, which has been likened to the scene under Juliet's window, climaxes in the solemn promise "Not a hair of your head shall be touched as long as I live!" (164), by which Lingard binds himself to a course of action that jeopardizes the interests of the young Malays. The events of the following chapters—the kidnapping of the two gentlemen, the complications communicated in the letter from Joergenson, Lingard's confused state of mind as the yacht people transfer to the brig, and the movements of Daman as shown in the conversation between Lingard and the *serang* Wasub—further build up the tension and prepare for the crisis that the enactment of that promise will bring in the life of Lingard.

Part four bears the suggestive title "The Gift of the Shallows." In light of the symbolic implications of the opening of part two, this title should head the three remaining parts. The increased importance of romantic love in the book may be held responsible for the fact that it does not. The first chapter in which Edith Travers declares that she expects "everything" from Lingard as he transports her from the *Hermit* to the *Lightning*, is pitted against chapter four of part two in which Lingard came to understand that the young people he has taken under his wings expect "everything" from him. His mental state of perplexity increases with the arrival of the Malay and Hassim's report in the following chapter. Meanwhile Edith Travers and Immada come to the clear recognition of the situation as being a contest between them for the loyalty of Lingard.

Edith Travers is determined to win; therefore she stays near Lingard on the trip to the *Emma* and later to Belarab's stockade. With the arrival of Immada on the *Emma*, the contest continues for the two women whereas for Lingard the outcome has been decided in the previous chapter, and the remaining two parts of the book center therefore on the conflict not between friendship and love but between that of his infatuation and his sense of honor, which obliges him to save the woman's husband.

The heading of part five is accordingly "The Point of Honor and the Point of Passion." The time shifts which occur after chapter one has shown the Travers on the *Emma* and their physical accommodation there has been made known, bear the mark of the years that had elapsed before these parts were written. They are more sophisticated inasmuch as the turn to retrospective narrative is led up to indirectly and the information which is expected from it is delayed. The resulting complicated narrative demands the reader's constant close attention, and the sense of frustration that nevertheless may build up is a consequence of the fact that temporarily the author himself has lost sight of the time scheme. In its total effect, however, the result reflects the confused state of mind of the protagonist.

The labyrinth into which the reader is led begins early in chapter two with the following observation: "The only time when Lingard had detected something of a deeper comprehension in d'Alcacer was the day after the long negotiations inside Belarab's stockade for the temporary surrender of the prisoners" (280). The reader expects that in the subsequent narrative some evidence be provided as to the manner in which Lingard gained that assurance. Instead there follows an account of Belarab's position as a leader of the settlement, his escapes and frustrations, and Lingard's view of his own chances with that ally. From there the narrative turns to the afternoon of the day on which he and Mrs Travers have arrived on the *Emma* and on which, in a lengthy, perplexed discourse Lingard has presented the difficulties of the situation to Edith. Without any suggestion of a time shift, the omniscient narrator unfolds the resulting mental state of the lady who wishes to have been left in the dark or to be able to share Lingard's confidences with d'Alcacer. With this the reader suddenly is back in time and place with Edith Travers at the end of chapter one; the time of the preceding reflections remains undecided.

This confusion continues in the following chapter. Still given to her mental preoccupations, Edith remains on deck while her husband and d'Alcacer enter the "Cage." Then she is the cause of a surprising communication that confuses the time scheme still more. "Since *that afternoon* when the gentlemen, as Lingard called them, had been brought on board, Mrs Travers and Lingard had not exchanged one significant word" (286, my italics). Following this statement comes a longer stride backward to the time before the negotiations in Belarab's camp when Edith Travers had declared that she would accompany Lingard and Joergenson to the crucial meeting and the former had invested her in the garments intended for Immada. A detailed account of the negotiations with Daman ends with the transfer of the prisoners to the *Emma*. Thus the chapter is brought to an end without having revealed how Lingard had "detected something of a deeper comprehension" in d'Alcacer.

Neither do the following chapters provide the expected information. Rather, a lengthy conversation of Edith and Lingard and of the lady with d'Alcacer follow. Then chapter three ends with the explosive news that with the destruction of the praus of the Illanuns by Carter the pact with Lingard's allies is broken. The earlier presentation of Daman as an essentially insecure person has prepared for the seriousness with which that news is viewed and explains the state of shock in which Lingard is shown when he speaks to Edith in chapter four.

These additional complications find expression in a complicated series of time shifts in chapter five. It opens with the day when the two gentlemen were transferred to the *Emma* and Hassim and his sister set out to Belarab's camp. Then it briefly moves back to the achievements of Jaffir, who has stopped the first officer of the yacht on his mission to find help in the straits, to Jaffir's return to the *Lightning* and his subsequent arrival on the *Emma* with the explosive message from Carter and then, following a lengthy conversation with Lingard, to his departure to find his prince. A further flashback communicates the sentiments that moved Lingard to impart the alarming news to Edith Travers after he had informed Joergenson. Continuing the retrospective narrative, the reflections of d'Alcacer on the relation between Edith and Lingard are made known, and the morbid mental state of Mr Travers is revealed. The tense conference of Lingard with Edith, which closes the chapter in the simple past, ends in the mutual understanding that the prisoners have to be returned to the Malays without any delay, if a chance for saving them should be secured. The final chapter continues the narrative in the simple past, telling the effect of this intelligence on Travers and d'Alcacer and their departure to the settlement while Edith Travers remains on the *Emma* in a state of mental distraction.

Part six, "The Claim of Life and the Toll of Death," opens with the immediate foreshadowing of the final disaster by showing Joergenson's experiments in timing the burning of strings. After this the lot of the Malay friends is led up to with Jaffir's flight with the emerald ring, which is followed by a flashback that shows their capture by Tengga's warriors. Chapter two ends with the succinct communication that Carter has succeeded in setting the yacht afloat. The conference of Jaffir and Joergenson, which follows in chapter three, results in the reunion of Edith with the other Europeans as the bearer of Hassim's ring. Her earlier passionate appeal that Lingard should not come near her again and Joergenson's refusal to tell her the meaning of the ring cooperate into making the behavior of Lingard and Edith at her arrival in the stockade plausible, and thereby the tension and contrast between the general state of affairs and Lingard's state of mind in the following chapters is increased.

As if to allow for a recovery from the shock of the subsequent events, the narrative resumes only thirty-six hours later with the attempt of Carter to rouse his listless Captain. The *serang's* arrival to impart to Lingard what he has heard from the dying Jaffir builds up suspense because of the time shift that delays the eagerly expected information. It first takes the reader back to the night which Lingard has spent with Edith Travers in total oblivion of reality, then to the conference with Belarab, followed by a report on Tengga's activities, the explosion of the *Emma*, and the departure of the white people from Belarab's settlement. Only in chapter eight Wasub finally reports the account Jaffir has given on the things that meanwhile had happened on the *Emma*. With it the retrospective narrative comes to an end. Lingard's visit to the dying Jaffir and the concluding message from Hassim to Lingard to forget everything complete the framework of the structure of *The Rescue*.

As a result of the changes Conrad made in the text, the critic who hopes to disentangle the mixture of early and late qualities in the style of *The Rescue* is faced with some difficulty. More so since the long stride forward in the development of Conrad's narrative art from *Almayer's Folly* and *An Outcast of the Islands* to *The Rescue* is obvious from the earliest beginnings of the latter. Edward Garnett spoke of a "new note" of "clear realism" when in May 1896 he evaluated the first sample of this new fiction. Conrad achieved that change mainly by a new approach to the presentation of characters.

In some respects a similarity of the first parts of *The Rescue* with the previous novels is nevertheless undeniable. The most obvious ones are those qualities of Conrad's style that have been marked as shortcomings in the other two novels. Storms are again strongly relied on in the first parts of the novel to foreshadow events and to reflect mental states, and much direct description of the setting aims at creating atmosphere for a similar purpose. Despite his attempt to present characters from an inner perspective, there still are traces of his earlier heavy dependence on setting for achieving an understanding of the characters.

As a metaphoric image the Shore of Refuge foreshadows and interprets the development of the protagonist. "The wreckage of many defeats unerringly drifts into its creeks" (63). With this casual remark the reader is made to understand that Lingard's giving in to his passion for political adventure, which requires his becoming lawless, is a moral defeat. Soon the consequences become apparent. To the degree that the Shore of Refuge attracts Lingard, he is less of a friend to his former comrades; he becomes touchy and insecure and dependent on impulses and desires.

A subtle correspondence is also suggested between the way setting appears to Lingard at his approach to the Shore of Refuge and his inner condition. The undifferentiated outline of the Shore renders the approach hazardous; it is the objective correlative to his confused motivations that make him unable to see things clearly and complicate the process of making decisions. In a similar way, the appearance of enchantment and splendor of Belarab's settlement and its surrounding and the dangers hidden in it suggest the character of that politician who is misleading because of his insecurity joined with a pacifist attitude and who therefore is a dangerous partner. The "wrath and fire of Heaven" that threaten at Lingard's first and only visit to Wajo (80) are likewise charged with implied meaning, as the further events of Lingard's life suggest.

The qualities of Conrad's early style are unmistakable in passages such as the one which describes Lingard's experience of a sunset as he is about to approach the Shore of Refuge for the last time:

> The falling sun seemed to be arrested for a moment in his descent by the sleeping waters, while from it, to the motionless brig, shot out on the polished and dark surface of the sea a track of light, straight and shining, resplendent and direct; a path of gold and crimson and purple, a path that seemed to lead dazzling and terrible from the earth straight into heaven through the portals of a glorious death. (14)

The relationship between the symbolism of the effects of light, Lingard's ambitions, and the impending danger is obvious. For the sake of comparison, the following passage from the penultimate chapter of the book may serve to illustrate the author's late style:

> "The mist has thickened. If you see anything, Tuan, it will be but a shadow of things." . . . Lingard felt the draught of air in his face, the motionless mist began to drive over the palisades and, suddenly, the lagoon came into view with a great blinding glitter of its wrinkled surface and the faint sound of its wash rising all along the shore. A multitude of hands went up to shade the eager eyes, and exclamations of wonder burst out . . . (437, 440)

The fog, which shrouds the lagoon during the minutes preceding the explosion of the *Emma*, is a subtle device with a multiple function. It is the objective correlative to Lingard's mental state, which he himself sums up in the sentence, "I can think of nothing" (412). It also serves to build up suspense by the delayed disclosure of Tengga's activities, and it heightens the impact of the explosion by the concentrated attention which it causes among the onlookers.

The most significant advance over the state of his art in the earlier novels is Conrad's attempt to present psychologically convincing characters from the first start of "The Rescuer." All the information, especially that on the protagonist, aims at building him up from an inner perspective. "As to the 'lyri[ci]sm' in connection with Lingard's heart," Conrad wrote to Garnett, "That's necessary! The man must be episodically foolish to explain his action. But I don't want the word. I want the idea" (CL I 284).

In the early stages of the novel, Conrad repeatedly relied on his strength in description to reveal Lingard's psychology through physical characteristics. The result gives away the great effort which the author has made to let the reader perceive the qualities which he aimed to expose; as in the first two novels, a crowding of modifiers, repetition for emphasis, and excess in detail produce the impression of strain and belaboredness. The description of Lingard's eyes in "The Rescuer" may serve as an example. It is to prepare the reader for the impact visual impressions have on the protagonist, especially when he meets Edith Travers:

> The eyes gave the face its remarkable expression. The eyebrows much darker than the hair overhung them in a bushy growth below the high and unwrinkled brow of an uniform bronze tint. The eyes themselves were small grey, fixed with a changeless scrutinising expression that did not seem to vary with the play of features—with the change in the man's moods. They seemed to be purely instruments of vision, as unconscious of the heat within the man as a telescope is unconscious of the incomprehensible emotions of the hopes, of the strange exultation within the breast of an astronomer watching for a new planet. They seemed instruments powerful and indifferent, slow to move, quite immovable when once arrested—as unflinching, no matter what they had to see, as things perfect for their purpose, but without life, would be. The whites were slightly and permanently bloodshot. This did not as might have been the case give him a dissipated appearance; but only added another touch to the pervading and yet hardly definable strangeness of his aspect. (12-13)

In *The Rescue*, Conrad shortened this passage as follows: "The eyebrows, darker than the hair, pencilled a straight line below the wide and unwrinkled brow much whiter than the sunburnt face. The eyes, as if glowing with the light of a hidden fire, had a red glint in their greyness that gave a scrutinizing ardour to the steadiness of their gaze" (9-10). In this way, Conrad retained the important idea of Lingard's passionate nature betrayed in his eyes; but he dismissed the notion of their being unconscious instruments and enlarged the understanding gained in this way with the allusion to the symbolic significance of light and darkness in the novel. In this way he again prepared for the impending meeting with Edith Travers, in whose person the symbolism of light is of major importance.

A repeatedly employed device in the first half of *The Rescue*, which for the sake of consistency Conrad carried over into the parts that he added later, is the use of parallels. By the similarities and contrasts that are emphasised in that way, important mental and emotional states of the characters, as well as related functions and situations, are revealed or implicitly commented on. Besides the calms followed by storms, which suggest challenges to Lingard's plans and expectations as he approaches the Shallows and Wajo, there is the demonstration of his sensitivity towards his vessel to prepare for the recognition of the way Edith Travers affects him. Joergenson is recognized as the commentator on Lingard's political passion, as d'Alcacer functions as that on his passion for the English woman. Edith Travers expects "everything" from Lingard to balance the expectations of the fugitive Malays, and the fidelity of Jaffir as the follower of Hassim has its parallel in that of Wasub, the faithful *serang* of Lingard.

Mystification is a means by which in the early half Conrad attempts to convey a taste of the Malay context and of the shady nature of Lingard's affairs. The forces at work in him as he throws his whole existence into the preparation for war are to be understood against the Malay background of belief in the powers of superstition, magic, and ghosts. In the later half of the book, Conrad abandoned these means, but chance and coincidence, which are likewise frequently employed, remain important crutches throughout the novel.

Related to these is Conrad's heavy reliance on the element of time as a thematic and symbolic device in addition to the narrative function shown above. Thematically, it serves above all to prepare a frame of plausibility for the way their meeting affects Edith Travers and Tom Lingard. Edith's disillusionment with her husband followed promptly on her marriage. But it is only in the silence and isolation of the Shallows that the fact of its finality comes home to her as an experience of an unbroken night. Into this the lantern of Lingard's brig throws a ray of hope. Her romantic inclinations are stimulated by the personality of Lingard and dispose her to respond to his appeals the way she does. The susceptibility of Lingard to the promise of her personality is likewise activated by the way the circumstances under which they meet affect him. If chance is responsible for the convergence of the two vessels in the Shallows, the timing of crisis experiences accounts for the psychological conditioning that leads to the subsequent developments.

In its symbolic function, time is mainly an indicator and measure of Lingard's capacity to perceive and to respond to the realities of his life. While he is fully in touch with them, time is rigorously registered and mention of the time piece in Lingard's cabin is frequent (9, 14, 28, 41). The sunset occurs at three minutes past six; half an hour later it is dark (17); after dinner the mate is on deck again at eight (19), the Captain at half past eight (18); the storm hits the *Lightning* half an hour past midnight (46).

With the arrival of the brig in the Shallows, Lingard's attention shifts from his brig to the larger context and is preoccupied with the disturbing fact of the presence of the yacht where he does not want it to be. The lessening of his competency in coping with reality is reflected in the decreasing rigor in recording time; time designations become approximate: the arrival of the brig occurs at noon; Lingard's conflict with Mr Travers happens in the afternoon; dinner on the *Hermit* is served at sundown; and Lingard's return to the yacht as well as the kidnapping take place sometime after nine.

This lack of exact information increases with Lingard's infatuation. Tentatively the clock in his cabin functions as a corrective (171), but presently it remains disregarded and never is mentioned again. The night is crowded with important occurrances without any clue as to the hour at which they take place. Edith Travers and her people transfer to the *Lightning*; Lingard confers with her in his state room; Hassim arrives with his sister and reports on the goings-on in Daman's camp; all leave for the *Emma* and arrive there at daybreak.

With his separation from the brig, the loss of Lingard's hold on reality is complete; time references become confused and unreliable, and time pieces are out of order or absent. The watch of Mr Travers is broken (336), that of Lingard has stopped; as a "dead watch" it is good only for the sinister experiments of Joergenson with the timing of explosive devices (362, 364, 368), and the watch of d'Alcacer has been left behind on the yacht (337).

After their arrival on the *Emma*, Lingard declares to Edith, "While I was talking to you *that evening* from the boat it was already too late"

(250, my italics). The reader knows that only one night has passed since then, and although this time reference is possibly the consequence of a lapse in the attention of the author, it fully fits in with the general unreliability as to the informations on time in part five. For it is unlikely that Conrad intended to imitate Shakespeare's technique of simulating passage of time by the use of phrases such as "since that afternoon" (286), "how many days ago it was" (307), or "Hassim's daily speeches" (373), when at the same time there is evidence that the elapsed time does not cover a whole week.

Lingard's words to Edith Travers on the day when the message from Carter is received furnishes the clue. He tells her that two days are necessary for Belarab to return to the settlement (299). If two days are likewise allowed for Hassim and his sister to reach Belarab's camp, his words are spoken on the fourth or fifth day after his arrival on the *Emma*, which has been the day on which the two young people set out on their mission. Before the following morning, the prisoners are returned to Belarab's settlement and shortly after, on the same day, that man's arrival there is reported (369). The time of the subsequent events is again clearly recorded to effect the strongly ironic contrast between Lingard's befogged state of mind, to which he calls everyone's attention with his reference to clock time (415), and the threatening reality in the settlement.

As in the previous novels, night is the time at which the most significant events occur. It is night when Lingard rescues the Malays and thereby assumes the role of a political redeemer, when Belarab's decisive visit takes place that makes him and Lingard allies, when Carter arrives with the news about a stranded yacht, when the Europeans are kidnapped and Lingard pledges that Edith would not suffer harm, when he separates from the *Lightning*, when Jaffir arrives with the letter from Carter, when the gentlemen are returned to the power of the Malays, and when the Europeans depart from the settlement.

Night, however, is not identical with darkness. This Conrad emphasised with the change he made in the observation of Carter that night/darkness affect human beings. Whereas in "The Rescuer" the passage reads, "It struck him that darkness brings men to a lower level" (77), *The Rescue* has, "such a night brings men to a lower level" (43), which allows for nights illumined by stars and the moon. But in the nights of the direct action of *The Rescue* darkness prevails, as is suggested by the first mention of nightfall as a surrender to darkness: "darkness had taken complete possession of earth and heavens" (16-17).

The symbolic implications of darkness vary. When the brig is shrouded in darkness as Carter's boat arrives, when the squall hits it, and when later Daman's presence threatens it, it is a potential agent of danger, so much so that for a time it even stifles Carter's good humor (42). When Lingard approaches Wajo in consequence of which he starts on his lawless career, darkness is seen as hiding a beast of prey: "Hassim's native land seemed to leap nearer at the brig—and disappear instantly as though it had crouched low for the next spring out of an impenetrable darkness" (79).

More often, darkness suggests mental states of confusion, hopelessness, and a sense of guilt. So for instance, when Edith Travers speaks her "So be it!" the enveloping darkness corresponds with her inner disposition that sees her future as a "mute and smooth obscurity . . . hung before her eyes in a black curtain without a fold" (152). Darkness is identical with hopelessness also for Hassim and his sister when it closes in on them after Shaw expelled them from Lingard's cabin (240) and when after their capture by Tengga's men the narrator suggests that complete darkness was "a fit ending" to the conference of Jaffir and Joergenson on their cause (379). Significantly, Conrad speaks of the light from Lingard's ship as one of "forbidden hopes," which is an indirect comment on the Malays' desire for ties of friendship with the white man.

The words of Edith Travers to d'Alcacer, on whether he considers her as a "creature of darkness" (313), however, suggest a consciousness of guilt. Likewise the assurance of Lingard to her that he would not have spoken of his desire to live for her if there had been light in her cabin; therefore he repeatedly emphasises her innocence (355). But the "darkness of his regained life" to which Lingard awakens at the end of the novel suggests both, hopelessness and awareness of guilt (445).

Lingard's inner confusion is best made visible by the interplay of light and darkness when torches are lighted on the brig to receive the people from the yacht. Danger, uncertainty, and doubt struggle fiercely with reassurance and hope (192). This situation of extreme nervous strain reaches a climax when after the torches are extinguished the brig is enfolded by a dense darkness, while the light in the cabin is too brilliant to allow a clear recognition of details. Light and darkness cooperate into obscuring the facts of reality also when, in the company of Edith Travers, Lingard has the sensation that her laughter makes darkness "brilliant as day, warm as sunshine" (159) and when he puts "absurd hope" and "incredible trust" in her person (214). Her gesture of throwing away the burning torch at the sound of Lingard's voice as she approaches Belarab's stockade at night (393) harmonizes with the general presentation of Edith as being light and hope in the eyes of Lingard, a light, however, that in fact blinds him.

It is of significance that the explosion of the *Emma* happens neither in darkness nor in bright daylight but in the early morning. Dawn is the time of undecided possibilities. It is the time when the pair of young Malays is introduced (64), when the idea of a war on Wajo is formulated (92), and when the first encounter of Lingard and Belarab takes place (106). Despite the death of many, the destruction of the *Emma* is likewise not to be seen as an event of finality, but of the possibility of new beginnings. In light of Joergenson's earlier observation that all Lingard is "worth in this world" is on the *Emma* (172), this is a challenging offer as well as an eloquent comment on the value of a man that can be confined to a ship.

Like that of darkness, the symbolic function of light varies. It has been seen that to Hassim and his sister the light of Lingard's cabin means hope (240); that also is the message that Edith sees in the light on the fore-yard-arm of the brig as she follows a dark train of thought before the return of Lingard on the evening of their first meeting (152).

Mostly, however, light interferes with, rather than enhances, the perception of the reality that adheres to persons and things. It dazzles and blots out details. The description of Edith Travers whose dazzling complexion seems to "throw out a halo round her head" (139) and the scene in Lingard's stateroom lighted with an "extraordinary brilliance" (214) are the most extreme examples of Conrad's exploitation of the blinding effect of light to explain Lingard's inability to see aright and to make competent decisions. The mention of his eyes as giving his face its "remarkable expression" (9) and the comment of Immada that the eyes of Edith are "like rays of light" (242) correspond with the general importance of the symbolism of light and darkness.

Like the complexion of Edith, the sunshines are dazzling. With one exception, which shows Lingard conducting business to prepare for war (97), all occasions on which sunshine is mentioned refer in some way to Edith Travers: her hair (139), her laughter (159), her sensation on the boat going to Belarab's settlement (288), her impression of the scenery there after the negotiation for the temporary release of her husband (297), and her confrontation with uncertainty when she is left behind on the *Emma* (366).

The consistency with which the author reserved this word for references to Edith Travers also in the second half of the novel proves his effort to "catch on" to what he had done twenty years earlier. By the same token, it demonstrates the vast difference between his use of symbolism for characterization in the early and late period. Whereas the first two examples, taken from part three, aim at showing her personality and its effect on Lingard through physical qualities, all others reveal character by the mental and emotional states and processes in relation to which sunshine is mentioned. The first of the latter group, found at the end of the last chapter of part four, with which Conrad began the completion of the novel in his advanced age, is the key to all others. Watching the shore from the *Emma* shortly after her arrival there, Edith Travers sees it quivering in the sunshine "like an immense painted curtain lowered upon the unknown," and the Malay who walks on the seashore impresses her like a figure in an "Oriental tale" (260).

With this suggestive association to theater, play-acting, and fiction, Edith betrays her tendency to take for unreal whatever is strange and unknown to her. Retroactively, this insight explains the impact Lingard's story has on her early in the novel. "She forgot that she was personally close to that tale which she saw detached, far away from her, truth or fiction, presented in picturesque speech, real only by the response of her emotion" (163). Her emotional involvement is very limited, however, as later she admits saying, "I never forgot myself in a story" (302). In consequence, the element of unreality prevails and events become performances in which she acts a role or at which she is a passive onlooker.

Her romantic imagination provides for a variety of roles in which she experiences herself: that of a woman in a ballad (216), an actress in an exotic opera (295), a dreamer (391); and her outlandish appearance when she is dressed in the outfit intended for Immada further encourages and enhances her inclination toward play-acting.

In this way the author gradually lays open the ironic gap between what Edith appears to be, especially to Lingard, and what she is. Step by step, an impression of her personality is being built up by the authorial voice, by the opinion of d'Alcacer, by the opportunities to observe her relation to her husband and to see her interact with her European companions and the Malays, only to have it exposed as incorrect and misleading by the observations of another character, by the revelation of her thoughts and sensations, and by the objective interpretation of her conduct.

This presentation of character on different levels, one undercutting the claim to reliability of the other, has important thematic ramifications. The early mention of Edith's "dreams where the sincerity of a great passion appeared like the ideal fulfillment and the only truth of life" (151) and of her subsequent disillusionment at the discovery that her husband was "enthusiastically devoted to the nursing of his own career"

(152) dispose the reader to credit her with imagination and openness to possibilities beyond what is generally known and considered acceptable.

The Malay setting lays bare the pretensions inherent in the idea Edith has of herself. Since she does not understand the Malay language, it is only noise to her from which she protects herself by withdrawal into an emotional and mental isolation. From that safe distance she observes the manifestations of life as the scenes of a drama. This denial of reality is also one of responsibility and, consequently, also of sincerity.

In this way Edith Travers betrays her basic sameness with her husband. Although the latter accuses her of a lack of conformity, d'Alcacer calls her exceptional, and she herself claims to be unconventional, she is as much conditioned by the cultural and racial limitations of her European origin as Travers, in whose eyes it is "a gain" if the "inferior race" perishes (148). D'Alcacer confirms this with the remark that the Travers "are quite fit to understand each other thoroughly" (410). In saying so, he seems to contradict his own observation that there is an affinity between Edith Travers and Lingard "as if they had been made for each other" (310). But since to Lingard an opera is more real than actual life (301), he meets Edith on common ground. As the opera was the "most real" thing to Lingard, so Edith is most real to him, and the warning of d'Alcacer that he does not know women is altogether lost on him.

More even than in the earlier novels, the author provided opportunities for reader discovery in regard to the real character of Lingard by an untiring insistance on his simplicity. As with Edith Travers and d'Alcacer, early warnings are given not to take narrator information at its face value. The reader who is determined to discover the reality behind Lingard's apparent simplicity is assisted by the truthfulness which makes him betray his actual complexity. Both action and dialogue serve as gates to enter into the world of the protagonist's complex psychology without his own awareness of it. The fidelity with which Lingard acts out his cultural and psychological conditioning without knowing it, but also without being absolved from responsibility for the consequences, is the means by which Conrad enlists the reader's sympathy for the protagonist up to the very end.

Both the petering out of Lingard's enthusiasm for his political romance and the futility of his conviction that in Edith Travers he has found a friend are logical consequences of his taking for real what is a show in her. For to the degree that she not only assigns a role to Lingard in the drama of her own life, but looks at his problems as a stage show (282), she denies their reality and refuses to assume responsibilities.

In this way stage and play-acting evolve as a major device to make character known. In the case of Joergenson and d'Alcacer, the two commentators in the story, the connection is less obvious. Joergenson shows Conrad at his weakest and at his best. He is a failure when he is said to be incapable of sustaining a conversation and subsequently shown as having written a letter exhaustive in length and detail. But he is also a rewarding object for the study of psychological subleties and play-acting.

His strategy in sounding Lingard on his political project is a good example. Joergenson's tactics resemble those of Cassius towards Brutus in *Julius Caesar*. "The new Rajah Tulla smokes opium and is sometimes dangerous to speak to," he cautiously observes. "There is a lot of discontent in Wajo amongst the big people" (99). Taken by surprise, Lingard responds as Joergenson wanted him to, and with his repeated warnings to give up the dangerous game he elicits those responses from Lingard that furnish him with the desired information. Meanwhile the reader needs to keep in mind that Joergenson was "like a haunting spirit from the past *eager to step back* into the life of men" (98, my italics).

When he assumes the role of a commentator on Lingard's political project, play-acting becomes the key word: "what you can do is only child's play to some jobs I have had on my hands," he tells the younger man (100). Since Lingard is undeterred and Joergenson joins in the effort towards success, the task Lingard faces gradually appears in a different light; it is no "child's play" any longer (366). In this way Joergenson not only acknowledges his own return to the ranks of ambitious strugglers toward a goal, he also admits that earlier he has been play-acting, and simultaneously he comments on the attitude of Edith Travers who regards Lingard's affairs as a performance. By the general consistency of Joergenson in acting the ghost that has returned from the grave, however, the possibilities for further discoveries as to his character are precluded.

The function of d'Alcacer as a commentator on the relation of Edith Travers and Lingard, on the contrary, provides more surprises. The fact that he remains in the dark as to the nature of Lingard's dilemma on the one hand and the generally accepted opinion that he is fully detached from life—while he proffers evidence that he is not—on the other, bring about a subtle interplay of affirmation and ironic negation in the narrative voice. Since the reader's sympathy with this character of nobility and sensitivity is liable to interfere with the detection of his flaw, however, his opinions and comments tend to pass unexamined.

D'Alcacer functions much like the chorus in a Greek drama when he remarks that "there is liking at first sight . . . as well as love at first sight" (130) or when he states that "the world of dreams . . . [is] very dangerous" (314). He is a commentator also by what he appears to be—the equilibrium by which the passion of Lingard for Edith Travers and her romantic indulgences are set off. In some way, he functions as a "centre of calm" (Geddes 164) in the storm of emotions of the triangular relationship of Lingard and the Travers. By his freedom from the prejudices of class distinctions and national pride and by his generous allowances for the individualities and idiosyncrasies of his companions, he comments on the gap between what Mr Travers protests to be and what he is. The observation of the narrator that d'Alcacer is "more of a European than a Spaniard" (309) is balanced against the opinion Mr Travers has of him as a "mere Spaniard" with symptoms of a "decayed race" (271).

The comment of the narrator is intended as a compliment. In its actuality, however, it explains part of the reason why d'Alcacer is an unreliable commentator. He functions on the basis of the conventions of Europe's "good society" (280) in which "unemotional behavior" is the correct thing (345), and he shares the general belief in the superiority of its civilization, which he sees threatened by the Malays. His comments on Edith Travers betray the limitations to which he himself is subject.

The more serious cause of his unreliability, however, is his incomplete detachment, which in crisis situations makes him interfere with the course of action; in consequence, his comments are colored by subjectivity and his conduct becomes dubious. The fact is that on account of his apprehension of danger d'Alcacer triggers the series of events that end in the final disaster of the *Emma*, when he prompts Mrs Travers to use her charm on Lingard in order to dispose that man to be friendly towards the people on the yacht (143). D'Alcacer is fully aware of the duplicity of his role, and towards the end of the novel, in the face of threatening death, he confesses how much he, too, was play-acting in paying homage to Edith Travers. Women, he says, "lead a sort of ritual dance, that most of us have agreed to take seriously. It is a very binding agreement with which sincerity and good faith and honour have nothing to do. Very binding. Woe to him or her who breaks it. Directly they leave the pageant they get lost" (412). This is the most sincere and enlightening, but also the most ironic, comment on the society Lingard hoped to be associated with and on the things that happen to him in consequence of it.

As foiling contrasts to that society, Conrad shows the single-minded fidelity and absolute genuineness of Lingard's Malay friends and the followers Wasub and Jaffir. It is a proof of the wisdom Conrad had acquired by his experiences with the first two novels that he abstained from a detailed characterization of the Malays. They are mostly recognized in the singularity of their qualities through their interaction with Lingard, on whose development they comment by what they are. There is nothing of play-acting in their loyalty and readiness unto death. It is therefore fitting that the ring, the symbol of fidelity, be returned to them by Lingard, and when that is no longer possible, that it be tossed into the ever-changing and ever-constant sea.

CONCLUSION

A journey through the Lingard novels is likely to take the reader back to where the tour began—the "Author's Note" to *Almayer's Folly*. In it, Conrad has in an epigrammatic form expressed his conviction that independent from geographical factors humankind and the human condition are essentially the same in all corners of the world. If this is not a generally recognized truth, Conrad reasons, it is because of a common inability to see things correctly by distinguishing important details. Conrad's goal as a creative artist is to outline such details for the reader so that they should not pass unobserved.

The guiding question in an evaluation of the development of Conrad's art in the Lingard novels must therefore be, how in writing them Conrad attempted to make the readers see details of life in the Malay setting and to what degree he succeeded at it. From this follows the important question as to the insights he thereby transmits. It is clear that the reception of these novels cannot be the measure to decide the author's success or failure but the growth in sensitivity to a common bond with all humankind of those readers who approach the novels with an awareness of, and the willingness to explore, the author's intentions.

The details of the human reality which Conrad aimed to expose in the Lingard novels are conditioned by the common factor of a white man confronted with life in the Malay Archipelago. To the extent that they are repetitious they confirm and substantiate the understanding gained separately in each of the novels. But they also have a complementary effect brought about by the differences in shades and distinctness in each individual novel. Most of these are given with the author's growth as an artist and less concerned with philosophical content than inherent in the form by which ideas are expressed. A gradual increase in sophistication and indirectness is the most immediately obvious change from novel to novel.

The continuous effort that bore those fruits is noticeable within each individual novel. In narrating the simple story of Almayer, Conrad depended mostly on the effects of forecast and delay which he achieved by a frequent use of time shifts. The brief span of the direct action of this fiction did not allow for character development and despite repeated attempts at giving insight into the minds of leading characters, the reader mostly remains on the surface; they do not come alive.

There is an indication of Conrad's growing artistic awareness, however, as he advanced in the writing of the novel. In order to increase its general human appeal, he added to the significance of Almayer's daughter by making her the object of rivalry between father and lover. With the tension of the Almayer-Nina-Dain triangle, Conrad not only achieved some degree of complexity but also a wider stage for displaying his ideas on the role of the white man in a Malay environment. It is mainly through this added dimension of the half-caste daughter who has to choose between the values of a European father and an indigenous mother and lover that the novel becomes a valuable document on the imperial theme.

An Outcast bears all the marks of the tensions between Conrad's increased artistic sensitivity and an acute awareness of his insufficiency in implementing what he recognized as desirable in his fiction. Added to this was the dread of failing his readers. The wider scope of the novel allowed for more intricacy in the presentation of characters and relationships, and more is disclosed of the inner life of Willems than of the protagonist of *Almayer's Folly*. The novel gains especially in depth through its substructure of the Lingard-Abdulla rivalry on which the value of this novel from the aspect of imperialist concerns is based. Unfortunately, much of it is obscured in consequence of the author's increased attempt to make the reader see by the help of extensive and elaborate descriptions and by the effort to render the narrative mode a reflection of thematic complications. In its resulting ponderousness the novel is in effect also a reflection of the weight of doubts and uncertainties under which the author labored in creating it.

The success of *The Rescue* in transmitting Conrad's ideas on European imperialism and the place and image of the Malay world in relation to it is most obvious. So much so that repeatedly this piece of fiction has been seen as the only one of the three Lingard novels that rewards an investigation in this respect. The most immediately apparent reason is the choice of themes which necessitate that together with the protagonist the readers become clear about their own affiliations in this confrontation of East and West. In addition to the thematic explanation, there is Conrad's handling of the narrative scheme with its frequent exploitation of foiling contrasts and revealing similarities for the purpose of exposing details more clearly. But the novel's success is not less the result of the general improvement of Conrad's creative ability that enabled him to present more convincing characters. In their aspirations and conflicts their world comes alive for the reader in a way that it did not in the previous novels.

It does not seem that the many years that passed before Conrad finally completed *The Rescue* brought about a change in the substance of the things that he wanted his readers to see in this novel. However, it certainly changed the intensity with which he attempted to achieve the task. By choosing the easier way out of the dilemma of being caught between romantic love and friendship in allowing the protagonist to surrender to the former, Conrad precluded possibilities for a fuller and more satisfactory treatment of the Malay question. This would have involved a treatment of the economic aspect of Lingard's enterprise in Wajo as much as of the political one. For Hassim's chances in political leadership are bound up with his potential as an "ideal Wajo trader," as the narrative has made clear in the beginning.

Thus the fact emerges that in all three Lingard novels Conrad handles the theme of European involvement in third world countries by pairing the white trader in the Malay setting with an Asian counterpart, Almayer and Lingard with Abdulla in *Almayer's Folly* and *An Outcast of the Islands* and Lingard with Hassim in *The Rescue*. Inasmuch as the ultimate objective in pursuing trade interests is an increase of influence and power for the ones as for the others, their ambitions are the same. The large-scale expansion at which the Europeans aim finds a more modest equivalent in the goals of the inter-island politics of Arabs and Malays. To the degree that the direct self-assertiveness of the white men contrasts with Abdulla's sly modesty and Hassim's gentle patience, their ambitions differ in their mode of manifestation, not, however, in essence.

Both East and West are divided into rival camps; but here the author employs parallel situations to expose essential differences. The hostilities among the English and the Dutch are well known to the indigenous population, who exploit them for their own interests. The tensions among the Arabs and the Malays and the tribal differences between the latter are as much a reality as those among the Europeans. In their common strife against the forces from the West, however, Arabs and Malays are united. In *The Rescue*, the Illanuns are ready to support Lingard's project not so much for the sake of the ousted Wajo princess and prince as because it is to be a move against the consolidation of the whites in the area. With these the piratical tribe means to settle a heavy score, and when with the destruction of the *Emma* that hope is taken from them, Lingard is an enemy in their eyes as much as the other Europeans.

The taintedness of Lingard's motivations renders their suspicions justifiable. Neither his dream of being the founder of an Arcadia in Sambir nor that of establishing a political confederacy in Wajo is free from personal ambitions and interests. In all three novels the opening to the undoing of the white man is given with his imperfect dedication to the cause he means to serve. In addition to providing the example of Joergenson in *The Rescue*, Conrad has underscored this message with the warning that Wyndham gives in "The Rescuer."

If a lack of disinterestedness renders the paternalism of the white man suspect and his genuine care in the end ineffective, it undermines the preconditions for friendship between Europeans and Malays from the start. "After all, it was perhaps a great folly to trust any white man, no matter how much he seemed estranged from his own people." This reflection of Daman in *The Rescue* (296) summarizes the sentiments of the Malay characters in the three novels, except those of Hassim. In the divergence of this character from the general rule, Hassim becomes Conrad's eloquent mouthpiece proclaiming hopefulness despite the prevailing pessimism. The significant message of Hassim's example is that a basis of trust between Europeans and Malays can be established not because of the superior generosity of the former but because of the capacity for generous forgiveness of the latter. To the degree that the European partner is capable of acknowledging this truth and acting on it, there is a possibility for a coexistence based on respect for each other.

Not, however, for a friendship that presupposes the recognition of the partner's equality and allows for mutual freedom and independence. The general consciousness of the European as bearing the white man's burden on account of his superiority and the equally general need of the Malay to appropriate the well-meaning westerner interfere with any effort in that direction. In "The Rescuer" Conrad speaks therefore of "strange friendships" that the white adventurers entertained in the Malay Archipelago, and the career of Joergenson in *The Rescue* demonstrates the degree of self-emptying that such friendships required. This insight offers a clue to Joergenson's demand that Hassim and his sister be brought on board the *Emma*, which he intends to destroy. "Death amongst friends is but a festival," he says (422). Victimization in one form or another is the inevitable result of any attempt to establish ties of affection and love, and the message to leave the territory and to forget everything, which Hassim twice sends to Lingard, is therefore also that of Conrad.

Hassim is Conrad's clearest expression of his belief in a civilization of indigenous peoples. In "The Rescuer," Wyndham speaks the words which later are repeated in *Heart of Darkness*, that when looked at closely enough the external differences disclose the common humanity which manifests itself in "primitive virtues." In the three novels these are displayed in a variety of ways and forms. But Hassim's gentle patience and generous trust differ from the fierce self-control that Dain practices when he spares the life of Almayer, who has threatened to betray him to the Dutch pursuers or from the stout-hearted loyalty of Ali, who remains trustworthy when all others have changed camps in Sambir. As an "ideal Wajo trader" Hassim is genuine in his native characteristics and, as Conrad implies in a variety of ways, these do not exclude qualities that contrast the Malay favorably with the civilization that Lingard represents.

No matter, however, whether their virtues be crude or refined, Conrad suggests, always they witness to an inner strength by which the Malay sustain what is typically their own. Individuals and tribal entities may become victims to the superior physical strength of the westerners, as the careers of Mrs Almayer, Omar, and Daman illustrate. Insofar as the piratical activities of those people justify the lot they have met, the Europeans are gainers; but only temporarily, for in the long run the weapons of blood and tribal consciousness, which unite and defend the indigenous people, are stronger than those of the white men who are divided among themselves. Temporarily the spirit of the conquered may be stifled, but it is unbroken and able to bide its time till it can reassert itself.

Significantly, it is mostly through the female characters of the novels that this is brought about. Nina comes to appreciate the Malay portion of her parental heritage on account of the contrast between the fierce power of her mother's life force and her father's weakness. Aïssa is the partly unsuspecting instrument that helps Malay interests to reassert themselves. Immada lives on in her people's memory as a great fighter gifted with the art of magic, that is, with qualities by which representative members of the tribe distinguish themselves and which therefore have an inspiring and unifying effect.

It is mostly in relation to the first two of these women that Conrad frequently applies the modifier 'savage'. In consistency with the presentation of her brother's personality, Immada bears the marks of refinement and Conrad abstains from using that adjective for her. But she resembles her sisters in the earlier novels as she is as full of the fire of expectations towards life as they are and—in strong contrast to her brother—keenly sensitive to its promises and demands. Her exclamation "let them die!" in reference to the intruders of the yacht is as fierce an assertion of the desire to recover and protect the tribal interests of Wajo as those life manifestations that are called 'savage' in the other novels.

The implications are obvious. Throughout, Conrad's use of the word 'savage' proves his belief in an undimmed life force in the indigenous people. Women are in a special way its bearers and guardians. Inasmuch as it is presented as being at the root of their resilience to weakening influences, its desirability is acknowledged. This meaning of 'savage' is in direct contrast with readings that find in it racial designations and expressions of contempt and inferiority. The transtextual characterization of minor figures such as Almayer's headman Ali or the Chinese Jim-Eng are in line with interpretations that assert Conrad's freedom from racial prejudices.

When in writing his second and third novel Conrad returned to the Malay Archipelago as his chosen setting, he may not have realized the degree to which transtextuality was to support his effort to make the readers *see*. Neither can he have been altogether unaware of it. The life manifestations in the Malay environment, which he outlines in the novels, are consistent and increasingly distinct. Transtextuality adds a second and third dimension to the outlines of the individual novels and provides the reader with the texture and flavor of realistic experinces. The perception of the ironic role of the white man in the colonial setting increases with the degree to which the understanding of the Malay approach to life grows.

In this way the Lingard trilogy becomes a valuable document of the role of Europe in Southeast Asia without allowing room for despondency. Juxtaposed to the negative representations of the past are intimations of alternative forms of relations between peoples for the future. It is characteristic of Conrad's Polish heritage of hopefulness that it made him envision more positive ones. The dawn that he sees rising on the horizon of the imperialist world view of his time holds a promise of the coexistence of East and West based on trust and the willingness to offer and accept forgiveness.

WORKS CITED

Allen, Jerry. *The Sea Years of Joseph Conrad*. New York: Doubleday, 1965.

Ave, Jan B. and Victor T. King. *People of the Weeping Forest: Tradition and Change in Borneo*. Leiden: National Museum of Ethnology, 1986.

Boyle, Ted Eugene. *Symbol and Meaning in the Fiction of Joseph Conrad*. The Hague: Mouton, 1965.

Caserio, Robert. "The Rescue and the Ring of Meaning." Murfin, *Conrad Revisited* 125-49.

Curle, Richard. *Conrad to a Friend*. New York: Doubleday, Doran, 1928.

Curreli, Mario. "A Further Note on Captain Lingard." *Conradiana* 10 (1978): 167-8.

Ehrsam, Theodore G. *A Bibliography of Joseph Conrad*. New York: Metuchen, 1969.

Fleishman, Avron Hirsh. *Conrad's Politics: Community and Politics in the Fiction of Joseph Conrad*. Baltimore: Johns Hopkins UP, 1967.

Ford, Madox Ford. *Joseph Conrad: A Personal Remembrance*. New York: Octagon Books, 1965.

Garnett, Edward. Introduction. *Letters From Joseph Conrad 1895-1924*. Indianapolis: Bobbs-Merrill, 1928.

Geddes, Gary. *Conrad's Later Novels*. Montreal: McGill-Queen's UP, 1980.

Gordan, John Dozier. *Joseph Conrad: The Making of a Novelist*. New York: Russell & Russell, 1963.

Guerard, Albert J. *Conrad the Novelist*. Cambridge: Harvard UP, 1966.

Hawkins, Hunt. "Conrad and the Psychology of Colonialism." Murfin, *Conrad Revisited* 71-87.

Karl, Frederick. "Three Problematic Areas in Conrad Bibliography." Murfin, *Conrad Revisited* 13-30.

Keppel, Sir Henry. *The Expedition to Borneo of H.M.S. Dido; With Extracts From the Journal of James Brooke, esqu. of Sarawak*. New York: Harper, 1846.

McClure, John A. *Kipling & Conrad: The Colonial Fiction*. Cambridge: Harvard UP, 1981.

Mannoni, O. *Prospero and Caliban: The Psychology of Colonialization*. New York: Praeger, 1964.

Marle, Hans van. "Jumble of Facts and Fiction: The First Singapore Reaction to *Almayer's Folly*." *Conradiana* 10 (1978): 161-6.

Murfin, Ross C. ed. *Conrad Revisited: Essays for the Eighties*. Alabama: U of Alabama P, 1985.

Najder, Zdzislaw. *Joseph Conrad: A Chronicle*. New Brunswick: Rutgers UP, 1983.

Parry, Benita. *Conrad and Imperialism: Ideological Boundaries and Visionary Frontiers*. London: Macmillan, 1983.

Schwarz, Daniel R. *Conrad: Almayer's Folly to Under Western Eyes*. Ithaca: Cornell UP, 1980.

———. *Conrad: The Later Fiction*. London: Macmillan, 1982.

Sherry, Norman. *Conrad's Eastern World*. Cambridge: Cambridge UP, 1966.

Stewart, J.I.M. *Joseph Conrad*. New York: Dodd, Mead, 1968.

Watt, Ian. *Conrad in the Nineteenth Century*. Berkeley: U of California P, 1979.

Watts, Cedric. *The Deceptive Text: An Introduction to Covert Plots*. Brighton, Sussex: The Harvester Press, 1984.

Wiley, Paul. *Conrad's Measure of Man*. Madison: U of Wisconsin P, 1954.

Yelton, Donald C. *Mimesis and Metaphor: An Inquiry into the Genesis and Scope of Conrad's Symbolic Imagery*. The Hague: Mouton, 1967.

Zimmermann, Peter. "Joseph Conrads Suedostasienwerke: Probleme realistischer Gesellschaftanalyse im Zeitalter des Fruehimperialismus." *Zeitschrift fuer Anglistik und Amerikanistik* 24: 37-56.

BIBLIOGRAPHY

Primary Sources

Aubry, G. Jean. *Joseph Conrad: Life and Letters*. 2 vols. New York: Doubleday, 1965.

Briggum, Sue M. and Todd K. Bender. *A Concordance to Conrad's* Almayer's Folly. New York: Garland, 1978.

Bender, Todd K. *A Concordance to Conrad's* An Outcast of the Islands. New York: Garland, 1984.

————. *A Concordance to Conrad's* The Rescue. New York: Garland, 1985.

Conrad, Joseph. *Collected Edition of the Works of Joseph Conrad*. 21 vols. London: Dent, 1946-1955. This edition follows the pagination of the "Uniform" and "Medallion" editions.

————. "The Rescuer." London: British Museum, Ashley Library, Manuscript 4787.

Curle, Richard. *Conrad to a Friend*. New York: Doubleday, Doran, 1928.

Karl, Frederick R. and Laurence Davies, ed. *The Collected Letters of Joseph Conrad*. 3 vols. to date. London: Cambridge UP, 1983-.

Secondary Sources, Books

Allen, Jerry. *The Sea Years of Joseph Conrad*. New York: Doubleday, 1965.

Ave, Jan B. and Victor T. King. *People of the Weeping Forest: Tradition and Change in Borneo*. Leiden: National Museum of Ethnology, 1986.

Berthoud, Jacques. *Joseph Conrad: The Major Phase.* Cambridge: Cambridge UP, 1978.

Bolt, Christine. *Victorian Attitudes to Race.* London: Routledge and Kegan Paul, 1971.

Boyle, Ted Eugene. *Symbol and Meaning in the Fiction of Joseph Conrad.* The Hague: Mouton, 1965.

Brooke, Sir James. *Narrative of Events in Borneo and Celebes from the Journals of James Brooke.* Ed. R. Mundy. 2 vols. London: John Murray, 1848.

Cox, C.B. *Joseph Conrad: The Modern Imagination.* London: Dent, 1974.

Daleski, H.M. *Joseph Conrad: The Way of Dispossession.* London: Faber, 1977.

Darras, Jacques. *Joseph Conrad and the West: Signs of Empire.* London: Macmillan, 1981.

Echeruo, M.J.C. *The Conditioned Imagination from Shakespeare to Conrad: Studies in the Exo-cultural Stereotype.* London: Macmillan, 1978.

Ehrsam, Theodore G. *A Bibliography of Joseph Conrad.* New York: Metuchen, 1969.

Fleishman, Avron Hirsh. *Conrad's Politics: Community and Politics in the Fiction of Joseph Conrad.* Baltimore: Johns Hopkins UP, 1967.

Ford, Madox Ford. *Joseph Conrad: A Personal Remembrance.* New York: Octagon Books, 1965.

Garner, Shirley Nelson et al. ed. *The (M)other Tongue: Essays in Feminist Psychoanalytic Interpretation.* Ithaca: Cornell UP 1985.

Garnett, Edward. Introduction. *Letters from Joseph Conrad 1895-1924.* Indianapolis: Bobbs-Merrill, 1928.

Geddes, Gary. *Conrad's Later Novels.* Montreal: McGill-Queen's UP, 1980.

Gekoski, R.A. *Conrad: The Moral World of the Novelist.* London: Paul Elek, 1978.

Glassman, Peter J. *Language and Being: Joseph Conrad and the Literature of Personality.* New York: Columbia UP, 1976.

Goonetilleke, D.C.R.A. *Developing Countries in British Fiction.* London: Macmillan, 1977.

Gordan, John Dozier. *Joseph Conrad: The Making of a Novelist.* New York: Russell & Russell, 1963.

Green, Martin. *Dreams of Adventure, Deeds of Empire.* London: Routledge and Kegan Paul, 1980.

Guerard, Albert J. *Conrad the Novelist.* Cambridge: Harvard UP, 1966.

Hay, Eloise Knapp. *The Political Novels of Joseph Conrad: A Critical Study*. Chicago: Chicago UP, 1963.

Howe, Irving. *Politics and the Novel*. New York: Horizon Press, 1957.

Howe, Susanne. *Novels of Empire*. New York: Columbia UP, 1949.

Hubbard, Francis A. *Theories of Action in Conrad*. Ann Arbor: UMI Research Press, 1984.

Johnson, Bruce. *Conrad's Models of Mind*. Minneapolis: U of Minnesota P, 1971.

Karl, Frederick. *Joseph Conrad: The Three Lives, A Biography*. New York: Farrar, Straus, and Giroux, 1979.

Kemp, T. *Theories of Imperialism*. London: Dobson Books, 1967.

Keppel, Sir Henry. *The Expedition to Borneo of H.M.S. Dido; with Extracts from the Journal of James Brooke, esqu. of Sarawak*. New York: Harper, 1846.

Klein, Fritz, ed. *Neue Studien zum Imperialismus vor 1914*. Berlin: Akademie Verlag, 1980.

Land, Stephen K. *Conrad and the Paradox of Plot*. London: Macmillan, 1984.

Lee, Robert F. *Conrad's Colonialism*. The Hague: Mouton, 1969.

McClure, John A. *Kipling & Conrad: The Colonial Fiction*. Cambridge: Harvard UP, 1981.

Mann, Thomas. *The Living Thoughts of Schopenhauer*. New York: Longmans, 1939.

Mannoni, O. *Prospero and Caliban: The Psychology of Colonialization*. New York: Praeger, 1964.

Marryat, Frank Samuel. *Borneo and the Indian Archipelago*. London: Longman, Brown, Green and Longmans, 1848.

Memmi, Albert. *The Colonizer and the Colonized*. Boston: Beacon Press, 1965.

Meyers, Jeffrey. *Fiction and the Colonial Experience*. Ipswich: The Boydell Press, 1973.

Miller, Hillis J. *Poets of Reality*. Oxford: Oxford UP, 1966.

Moser, Thomas. *Joseph Conrad: Achievement and Decline*. Cambridge: Harvard UP, 1957.

Murfin, Ross C. ed. *Conrad Revisited: Essays for the Eighties*. Alabama: U of Alabama P, 1985.

Najder, Zdzislaw. *Joseph Conrad: A Chronicle*. New Brunswick: Rutgers UP, 1983.

Nettels, Elsa. *James and Conrad*. Athens: U of Georgia P, 1977.

Palmer, John. *Joseph Conrad's Fiction: A Study in Literary Growth*. Ithaca: Cornell UP, 1968.

Parry, Benita. *Conrad and Imperialism: Ideological Boundaries and Visionary Frontiers*. London: Macmillan, 1983.

Raskin, Jonah. *The Mythology of Imperialism*. New York: Random House, 1971.

Roussel, Royal. *The Metaphysics of Darkness*. Baltimore: Johns Hopkins UP, 1971.

Said, Edward. *Joseph Conrad and the Fiction of Autobiography*. Cambridge: Harvard UP, 1966.

Saveson, John E. *Conrad, The Later Moralist*. Amsterdam: Rodopi N.V., 1974.

Schwarz, Daniel R. *Conrad:* Almayer's Folly *to* Under Western Eyes. Ithaca: Cornell UP, 1980.

———. *Conrad: The Later Fiction*. London: Macmillan, 1982.

Sherry, Norman. *Conrad's Eastern World*. Cambridge: Cambridge UP, 1966.

———, ed. *Conrad: The Critical Heritage*. London: Routledge and Kegan Paul, 1973.

Showalter, Elaine, ed. *The New Feminist Criticism: Essays on Women, Literature, and Theory*. New York: Pantheon, 1985.

Stallman, R.W., ed. *The Art of Joseph Conrad: A Critical Symposium*. East Lansing: Michigan State UP, 1960.

Stewart, J.I.M. *Joseph Conrad*. New York: Dodd, Mead, 1968.

Street, Brian V. *The Savage in Literature: Representations of 'primitive' society in English fiction 1858-1920*. London: Routledge and Kegan Paul, 1975.

Thornton, A.P. *Doctrines of Imperialism*. New York: John Wiley, 1965.

Watt, Ian. *Conrad in the Nineteenth Century*. Berkeley: U of California P, 1979.

Watts, Cedric. *The Deceptive Text: An Introduction to Covert Plots*. Brighton, Sussex: The Harvester Press, 1984.

Wiley, Paul. *Conrad's Measure of Man*. Madison: U of Wisconsin P, 1954.

Winks, Robin, ed. *The Age of Imperialism*. Englewood Cliffs: Prentice-Hall, 1969.

Wright, Walter F. *Romance and Tragedy in Joseph Conrad*. New York: Russell & Russell, 1966.

Yelton, Donald C. *Mimesis and Metaphor: An Inquiry into the Genesis and Scope of Conrad's Symbolic Imagery*. The Hague: Mouton, 1967.

Articles

Bonney, William W. "'Eastern Logic under My Western Eyes': Conrad, Schopenhauer, and the Orient." *Conradiana* 10 (1978): 225-52.

Curreli, Mario. "A Further Note on Captain Lingard." *Conradiana* 10 (1978): 167-8.

Geddes, Gary. "Clearing the Jungle: The Importance of Work in Conrad." *Queen's Quarterly* 73 (1966): 559-72.

Hammer, Robert D. "Joseph Conrad and the Colonial World: A Selected Bibliography." *Conradiana* 14 (1982): 217-229.

Hicks, John H. "Conrad's *Almayer's Folly*: Structure, Theme, and Critics." *Nineteenth Century Fiction* 19 (June 1964): 17-31.

Karl, Frederick. "Joseph Conrad's Literary Theory." *Criticism* 2 (1960): 317-35.

Lester, John. "Conrad and Islam." *Conradiana* 13 (1981): 163-179.

Lombard, Francois. "Conrad and Buddhism." *Cahiers Victoriens et Eduardiens* 2 (1975): 103-12.

McLauchlan, Juliet. "Almayer and Willems—'How Not To Be'." *Conradiana* 11 (1979): 112-141.

Marle, Hans van. "Jumble of Facts and Fiction: The First Singapore Reaction to *Almayer's Folly*." *Conradiana* 10. (1978): 161-6.

Moser, Thomas. "'The Rescuer' Manuscript: A Key to Conrad's Development and Decline." *Harvard Library Bulletin* 10 (autumn 1956): 325-55.

Nettels, Elsa. "James and Conrad on the Art of Fiction." *Texas Studies in Language and Literature* 14 (1972): 529-44.

Thomson, George H. "Conrad's Later Fiction." *English Literature in Transition* 12 (1969): 165-74.

Zimmermann, Peter. "Joseph Conrads Suedostasienwerke: Probleme realistischer Gesellschaftanalyse im Zeitalter des Fruehimperialismus." *Zeitschrift fuer Anglistik und Amerikanistik* 24: 37-56.

INDEX